UnLove invites its readers to rethink and revisit what they believe about their core identities and what it means to love others well. You will discover the journey of healing and transformation that empowered the author to live above his circumstances through the power of forgiveness, repentance, and reconciliation. Your identity is not shaped by what you have done or what was done to you. Your life matters to God and you were created to receive His love and to be an expression of grace and mercy to everyone you meet.

Dr. Ron Hitchcock

Author of "Journey to Oneness" and "Parenting Your Children into Adulthood"
Marriage and Family Pastor, Vineyard Columbus | Columbus, Ohio
President, Life In Motion Relationship Resources
www.VineYardComlubus.org | www.LifeInMotionResources.com

Thought-provoking. Genuine. Convicting.

Pastor Thomas Bush

Lead Pastor, Bayside Baptist Church | Superior, Wisconsin
www.BaysideSuperior.org

The practical wisdom and biblical application that is offered in this book will prove to be beneficial in whatever relational challenges you face.

Eric Rozeboom

President, Alaska Bible Institute | Homer, Alaska
www.AlaskaBible.org

I love that Nathan is constantly bring us back to that spectacular truth that we are set free to live a free life — it's already ours, yet we're still attaining it. READ THIS BOOK — and learn how to live out a full life in Jesus with others. It's possible — and God's desire for you!

Pastor Scott Frerking

Lead Pastor, Hill Country Fellowship Church | Burnet, Texas
www.HCFBurnet.org

UnLove has helped me to more deeply engage in the healing and sanctifying work that Jesus is doing in my life. Its practical and extensive approach has helped me to grow in my understanding and experience of what it means to be loved and to love.

Pastor Jesse Jorgensen
Associate Pastor of Worship, East Hills Alliance Church | Kelso, Washington
www.EastHillsAlliance.org

It's not often that you find a book that so eagerly beckons you into the messy, hard work of absolute forgiveness. Simple, powerful, real-world examples sparkle with truth and humor. *UnLove* takes you on the wild adventure of pursuing new heights in your relationships. Read this book with a pen in hand and readiness for growth. If you do, what you discover could absolutely transform your life.

Sarah Bultman
Christian Life Coaching
www.BirchRise.org

Dedicated in his personal journey towards wholeness and life-giving behaviors, *UnLove* reveals the lessons Nathan has learned to develop healthy relationships, combined with wise and practical steps, so that we can do the same.

Pastor David Pepper
President, Amazon Outreach
www.AmazonOutreachPeru.org

I cannot recommend this book enough! Following the tools and guidelines so clearly laid out in this book became the basis for my own freedom and healing. Walking through this book will open your eyes to the nuances of relationships you may never have considered. It is both a practical and spiritual guide for the two greatest commandments — love the Lord your God and love your neighbor as yourself.

Chelsea Weisser
Wife and Mom

We're made to live in wholeness, peace, and intimacy with God. The tools in this book can change your life and lead you there.

Shannon Guerra

Author of "Upside Down" and "Oh My Soul"
www.ShannonGuerra.com

UnLove is a great read with many years of research and teaching in every chapter. It helps us to understand how our hearts have gotten stuck, bitter, broken, bruised, or jaded, and shows us the necessary steps and paths out of our destructive coping habits. With the Word of God, practical wisdom, and vulnerability, Nathan takes us on the journey toward freedom. He is shifting our culture toward freedom.

Cate Morris

Evangelist, Author of "Beyond the Siege"
www.CateMorris.com

I have never been more excited to live free as when I read this book. Such a beautiful and thorough description of forgiveness and what it looks like to live in our true identity; believing who God is, and therefore, believing what He says about me is true and living in that identity. You will be challenged but encouraged at the same time. This book is anointed by the Holy Spirit who is able to accomplish it all in and through you.

Sarah Frerking

Pastor's Wife and Mom to Five Children

UnLove is an important book for this generation. It has been birthed out of great difficulties, which makes the impact of it even more significant. I know the heart Nate and Lacey have for people being made whole. Their journey to love is on display for us to witness and learn from. You will be encouraged, challenged, and blessed by reading this beautiful book of truth. The key to life is relationships and this book unlocks many deep and timeless truths of living free in relationship with God and others. I am excited to highly endorse this book and this couple.

Pastor Mark Pavola

Lead Pastor, Hope City Church | Duluth, Minnesota
www.HopeCityChurchDuluth.org

UN*LOVE*

UN*LOVE*

A BOOK ABOUT UNLEARNING AND
RESHAPING WHAT YOU KNOW ABOUT
GOD, LOVE, PEOPLE, AND RELATIONSHIPS

NATHAN STEEL

UN*LOVE*

A BOOK ABOUT UNLEARNING AND RESHAPING WHAT YOU KNOW ABOUT GOD, LOVE, PEOPLE, AND RELATIONSHIPS

Cultivate PUBLISHING

Learn more about Cultivate at: **www.CultivateRelationships.com**

To my wife, Lacey, for always sticking
with me, believing in me, encouraging me, and helping me
become a better person and communicator.

This book would not exist without you.
No words can express the gratitude I have toward you for
all you have given up and sacrificed for me.

ACKNOWLEDGEMENTS

I want to thank my good friend, Michelle, for editing this book. Your dedication, faith, and encouragement throughout the process of writing kept me focused and determined to see this project through to the end. Thank you for your love, support, and commitment to me and my family.

//

I also want to thank Shannon, who gave this project her final editing touches. I deeply appreciate you taking the many hours it took to read and edit this book.

//

One final thank you goes to Chelsea, my sister-in-law. I'm incredibly grateful to you for checking continuity and your invaluable advice. But most importantly, for your continued faith and support to my family!

TABLE OF CONTENTS

YOU'RE JUST NOT DOING IT RIGHT...
(the introduction)

I WAS THE BEST PARENT I KNEW OF... UNTIL I HAD CHILDREN.

We can often feel like we are experts at something until we recognize how little we actually know. For example, I remember thinking after adopting our first daughter that parenting was super easy. She was a quiet and easy-going toddler. We could read parenting books and perfectly implement the principles. After a few months of becoming a dad I remember judging other parents who had more stubborn children and thought, *they're just not parenting right. Cause, if they were, then their kids would be obedient like my daughter.*

Then we adopted our second daughter... and I had to grovel at the feet of Jesus, pleading him to forgive me for judging other parents so harshly.

Our second daughter is incredibly strong-willed, independent, and has the incredible gift of negotiation. We genuinely see these attributes as being from God. Therefore, rather than simply crushing her spirit, we are constantly having to trust the Holy Spirit to lead and guide us. This can often lead to feeling exhausted, unsure, and overwhelmed. And if you're thinking, *yeah, but you're just not doing it right.* You would probably be right.

When it comes to relationships, we can often feel like we know what we're doing and that we have it under control (or, maybe you feel completely out of control). Whatever the case, I'm willing to bet that you believe whatever difficulties you face in relationships would all be resolved if the *other person* would just change.

The reality is, we are all the *other person.* We are all learning what it means to be in healthy relationship with God and others.

Relationships — whether it's family or friends — are meant to be the most fulfilling aspect of our lives. Unfortunately, they can also be the most difficult, frustrating, disappointing, and stressful aspects of our lives. They require constant time, energy, work, and flexibility just to maintain. They need far more if we want those relationships to grow and flourish. While God designed us for connection, we will spend the rest of our lives learning how to cultivate healthy relationships. Whether you feel far from God or like you have a vibrant relationship with Him, the practical steps and resources in this book can help you become a more mature person in your relationships.

I was born with a genetic disease called cystic fibrosis. This disease led to lung infections that required me to spend a lot of my childhood in the hospital. I spent months away from my family, building friendships with kids my age who also had terminal diseases. Over the years, these friends eventually died and the friends I had when I was home didn't have any health issues; these factors combined left me feeling alone and unknown. I learned that if I didn't get close to people, I wouldn't get hurt. So, when my wife and I first got married, she would lovingly refer to me as "Fort Knox," meaning, I wouldn't let my thoughts and feelings be known and I would guard myself from other people getting too close to me.

Isolating myself from people led to a 20-year addiction to pornography. To further complicate our marriage, Lacey struggled with fear that fed an explosive anger. This produced in her a need to control me and our circumstances. As you can imagine, our inability to communicate and resolve conflict led to a breakdown in our relationship. Within a few short years we realized that, while we knew we wanted to be in relationship with each other, we didn't know how. We knew that for our marriage to survive (let alone, thrive) we would need help. We eventually made the decision to abandon our dreams of working in ministry to pursue counseling. This pursuit moved us away from our friends and family to a new community. While this sacrifice was painful, achieving wholeness in our marriage took over eight years and led to the adoption of our two girls, Lydia and Arianna.

The experiences we've had in our marriage have taught us that healthy relationships take time, effort, sacrifice, and communication. This book, and the principles found in it, were developed out of our own painful journey from isolation and anger to relational wholeness. We've worked with both individuals and couples and have seen people set free from lifelong anger and bitterness, estranged family members reunited, and those paralyzed by fear and anxiety become vibrant faith-filled risk takers.

The journey to personal and relational wholeness is one that requires the help and involvement of other people. We are designed to mature physically, mentally, and emotionally within the context of relationships. This process moves us from dependence upon others to interdependence with others. Our **dependence** is *a time frame in which we are solely reliant upon another person (or people) for our physical, mental, emotional, or spiritual well-being.* A few examples of healthy dependence are: 1) a baby depends upon its parents for food, shelter, love, and care; 2) someone recovering from a medical procedure may depend upon a loved-one for care and meeting their basic needs through recovery; 3) or we may need to depend upon a counselor for a time to help us emotionally or mentally. Our **interdependence** is *being fully confident in our own identity while comfortably relying upon the input, support, and involvement of another person (or people) for our continued maturity and well-being.* An example of this is a friendship where both people respect the time and personal goals of the other person while continuing to develop the friendship. They are individuals with separate lives and responsibilities, but they also make time for each other to mutually encourage and support one another.

Our interdependent relationships will promote freedom, vulnerability, and intimacy that lead to the growth of each person within the relationship. In these healthy relationships there will be mutual respect, trust, and support for each other's personal goals while still being committed to the other person. An interdependent person will act in the other person's best interest — giving room and encouragement for them to grow and express their own individuality. While it is God's design for us to be interdependent people, it is not something that comes naturally to us — it takes developing abilities, maturity, and understanding. When we are born, we are marked by immaturity, inability, and ignorance. This is not bad and is part of the process God designed. For us to mature, maturity must be demonstrated; for our abilities to grow, they need to be encouraged; and, for us to grow from ignorance to understanding, we must be taught. This entire process of development — physically, mentally, emotionally, and spiritually — is inherently linked to others.

From our birth, God designed and positioned us to trust and rely on others to meet our physical, mental, emotional, and spiritual needs. Our hearts are free to love and be loved by God and others. This ability to thrive in healthy relationships comes from our experiences in our early growing up years. However, if there is conflict in our developmental process, we become inclined toward mistrust and distrust, causing us to develop physical, emotional, mental, and spiritual insecurity. Unfortunately, for us to gain some sense of security, we become self-focused, self-reliant, and self-gratifying. While this may be a necessary response to unsafe, unloving, and unhealthy circumstances, it can have a negative long-term impact on our maturity. As we begin to look to ourselves (or someone else) exclusively to meet our needs, we become numb to the Holy Spirit's voice in our life. This is how we reject or neglect our God-given design and desires; they become inclined toward unnatural cravings and we enslave ourselves to unhealthy mindsets and behaviors.

Regardless of our age (physical maturity) or how long we have been a Christian, our emotions, thoughts, and spirit may remain immature. This immaturity is often revealed by our need to be independent or co-dependent in our relationships. **Independence** is *the belief that we do not need anyone, nor is our physical, mental, emotional, or spiritual well-being influenced by another person's behavior toward us.* I have often struggled with being independent. Since I spent a lot of my childhood in the hospital by myself and had to care for myself, I developed a self-focused mindset. *I am* the one who orders my medication. *I am* the one who does my respiratory treatments. *I am* the one solely responsible for my health. This led to me feeling like I don't need people or only using them to my benefit. Believing we are capable of functioning independent of God and others results in self-reliant (and often, judgmental) mindsets and behaviors. The Bible refers to independence as "pride" (James 4:6-7 and 1 Peter 5:5-7). Independency rejects God's grace — His personal attention, help, and support. It ultimately leads to us feeling misunderstood and others feeling pushed away.

Co-dependence is *the belief that our physical, mental, emotional, and spiritual well-being is totally and irrevocably connected to another person's behavior toward us.* A co-dependent person often unnecessarily or repeatedly checks in on their friend's availability or if there is "anything between them" that is causing them to not spend time together. They tend to lean on other people to feel important and valued. This can often leave a co-dependent person feeling insecure when someone hasn't returned a phone call or text in what they consider a "timely manner." When my wife struggled with co-dependency, she needed every argument to end in agreement or her being forgiven so she could move forward. She viewed her ability to be free and whole as dependent upon how others responded to her. Co-dependent people are driven by an intense compulsion to keep their every behavior guarded so as to not upset the people in their life. The Bible refers to co-dependence as "a fear of man" (Proverbs 29:25). Co-dependence fosters self-deprecating submission or suffocating manipulation and control of others to feel loved, important, or valued. It can leave people feeling smothered or manipulated.

Believing that co-dependency is healthy in our relationship with God will lead to a works and approval-based servant relationship — filled with exhaustive checklists, demands, and requirements that we can never live up to. Co-dependency can reject God-given personality traits (like goofiness, emotions, or stubbornness) as unnecessary or rebellious. It may also reject good and healthy desires meant for our joy and comfort (like sex, eating certain foods, or drinking certain beverages). These can become demonized by being viewed as ungodly or be abused in excess to cope with feelings of shame and guilt. Co-dependency in our relationship with God rejects His desire for us to be in a vibrant, co-laboring relationship with Him.

We often struggle with both independency and co-dependency to one degree or another depending on our relationships and circumstances. My goal in describing these unhealthy forms of relationships are not to label you with a false identity; rather, my hope is to reveal areas in your life where you may not be trusting the Holy Spirit.

God's goal for us is to be in an interdependent relationship with Him and others. While He is perfectly self-sufficient and needs nothing from us for His well-being, God invites us into a collaborative, symbiotic relationship that influences the outcome and actions of both Him and us. This mutually affecting relationship between God and us is marked by mutual respect and active ongoing communication.

——————— // ———————

I titled this book *UnLove* because I want to undo and reshape the preconceived ideas you may have about God, yourself, and relationships. Because our view of these subjects is often developed by how we were raised or what we are taught by trusted spiritual leaders, some of the subject matter may feel frustrating, heavy, or overwhelming at times. My challenge and encouragement to you is to set time aside each day to read, pray, and work through the activation steps at the end of each chapter.

Our past experiences influence our understanding of the world around us, so I'm not surprised if you come to this book with predetermined ideas and definitions. For this reason, I have highlighted and defined certain terms I feel are necessary to understanding the concepts I'm presenting.

I have found that how I react to difficult and stressful situations is often the result of my practiced reactions to normal, daily life. Therefore, some of the examples I use to help clarify certain points may appear to be generic, simplistic, or unrelated to your circumstances. My goal in highlighting these examples is to help you think through, value, and respond to the small moments in your life so you will know how to respond in the face of more serious situations.

My goal is that you would be encouraged — living confident in the tools you've been given to enjoy life and live connected in your relationship with God and others.

CHAPTER ONE

UNLOVE

UNLEARNING OUR
DEFINITION OF LOVE

[Christ] didn't, and doesn't, wait for us to get ready. He presented himself for this sacrificial death when we were far too weak and rebellious to do anything to get ourselves ready. And even if we hadn't been so weak, we wouldn't have known what to do anyway. We can understand someone dying for a person worth dying for, and we can understand how someone good and noble could inspire us to selfless sacrifice. But God put his love on the line for us by offering his Son in sacrificial death while we were of no use whatever to him.

— ROMANS 5:6-8, THE MESSAGE

MY SCHEDULE DOES NOT CHANGE. THIS IS ONE OF THE RULES I HAVE.

If I have something written down in my calendar, it does not change unless there is an extensive planning meeting to outline and detail what changes must be made to shift my schedule. If it were up to me, I would have the exact same meals planned out for the week. I would wear the same clothes every day. They wouldn't actually be the same clothes, but I would have the same style shirt, the same style pants, the same style socks, and the same style shoes. And my daily schedule blocks would be the same every day.

Some would say that I have obsessive-compulsive tendencies. I simply call it being structured and organized.

There is one issue I have in adhering to these "rules."

I have a wife.

My wife has rules as well. Her primary rule, however, seems to be interfering with my rules.

She is far more flexible in her schedule. In fact, she views schedules as restraints which hold her back from living in freedom. Her rule is that schedules should be avoided when possible.

We all have "rules" (i.e., expectations or assumptions) that we live by. These rules are imprinted onto our brains as we develop. They come through the relationships and experiences we have in our growing up years. Often, we don't even know we have a rule until someone breaks it. It is when we feel frustrated, disappointed, or offended that we recognize that we may have had a rule. And, once we deem someone as a rulebreaker, they can become more difficult for us to love.

———————— // ————————

God loves every person who has ever lived. And He has proved His love for us by extending the opportunity for reconciliation — being in relational unity with Him. He has thoroughly forgiven us for breaking relationship with Him through Jesus' death on the cross. This forgiveness is extended without any rules, assumptions, or expectations. God's only requirement for us is that we simply receive this forgiveness. Unfortunately, not everyone does.

We are empowered to walk in our God-given identity when we receive His forgiveness. This identity encourages healthy habits and behaviors that nurture a healthy relationship with Him and others. How we love and forgive others reveals how we believe God loves and forgives us. Therefore, the most revealing test of our love is our choice to thoroughly forgive others and our willingness to pursue relationship with them when possible.[1]

The freedom and grace that come with this forgiveness is the catalyst for encouraging a lifestyle of forgiveness. As we walk in step with the Holy Spirit, this choice to forgive and pursue relationship becomes easier and more natural.

LOVING MEAN PEOPLE

I love loving people who are easy to love. Loving them feel so easy. These are the people who generally follow my rules. They are people worthwhile to love because I usually get something out of it. And if they break my rules, I can simply fall out of love with them.

But Jesus tells us in Luke 6:27-35 that it is meaningless to love people who are easy to love. He challenges us to love those who offend us, disappoint us, and frustrate us. Also, these are the people who have affected us negatively. This can even be those we are loyal to and have no ill will toward. For the Jews Jesus was talking

---

[1] 1 John 4:7-21

to, the enemy was obvious. It was the Romans. Therefore, based on this context, Jesus is defining an **enemy** as *anyone who may have intentionally or unintentionally emotionally, physically, mentally, spiritually, sexually, or psychologically hurt, judged, manipulated, offended, used, or coerced us.* Basically, it is anyone who has distorted or devalued our perception of our identity through their words or actions. This sacrificial love Jesus describes even extends to areas of ourselves that we hate — aspects we view as unlovable or unworthy of love.

My biggest struggle in forgiving someone is that I am a grudge holder. I may not remember what I ate for breakfast, but I could tell you what someone said or did to me a decade ago. I remember offenses. I'm very black and white. It is easy for me to assign fault to someone along with identifying how they negatively affected me. My wife, Lacey, is an excellent forgiver. She forgives quickly and forgets quickly. This can make it difficult for her to assign fault to people and connect the negative affects they had on her because of her loyalty to them. My struggle to forgive comes from believing the person is undeserving of it. Lacey's struggle to forgive comes from not believing the person actually needs to be forgiven.

Our unwillingness to forgive trusts our own perspective of a person's character and motivation above what the Holy Spirit knows to be true of them. We either diminish or exaggerate the negative effects of a person's behavior on our mind and emotions. This leads to a belief that forgiveness is either unnecessary or undeserved. This unwillingness to pursue forgiveness rejects the Father's love, grace, and forgiveness.[2] We cannot extend to others what we have rejected, and therefore cannot experience, ourselves.

Forgiveness, on the other hand, trusts the Holy Spirit above our perceptions of people and their effect on us; it affirms that people's words and actions do affect our mind and emotions. Freedom from anxiety, fear, depression, and all the other unhealthy mindsets we have begins with our willingness to forgive. Our willingness activates God's grace to love, forgive, and release the

---

[2] Matthew 6:14-15

negative effects and the offender to Jesus. Furthermore, it allows the Holy Spirit to work our experience out for His glory and our good — replacing the bad with His good.[3]

> ## "How we love and forgive others reveals how we believe God loves and forgives us."

There is one person in my life who is a constant source of offense. The first time I was confronted about forgiving this person it took me six months to even be willing to say the words, "I forgive you." Nearly every conversation with this person leads to an "opportunity" to forgive. This person is one of the most difficult people I have had to be in relationship with.

It was about seven years after I had originally forgiven this person that I was asked to develop a New Believers class at the church our family attended. The purpose of the class was to teach new Christians important doctrines and how to apply them to their lives. The first time through the curriculum, the Holy Spirit gave me clarity as I was teaching the section on forgiveness. As I was talking, this phrase just popped out of my mouth: "We need to pursue relationship with difficult people because God wants to love them through us." Immediately after those words left my lips, I heard God speak to my mind, "That is what I am asking you to do with [this person]."

Forgiveness is the supreme test of love because it is the most selfless act we can do for others; it freely releases the offenders from a debt — an expectation or requirement — we believe they owe us when we pursue relationship with them. Our Heavenly Father loves us with an immeasurable, unconditional, never stopping,

---

[3] Romans 8:26-30; Ezra 8:22; Ecclesiastes 8:12; John 10:10

never giving up, always and forever love that He revealed in and through Jesus.[4] Forgiveness reveals our ability to truly understand and receive this love and extend that same love to others. It demonstrates our trust in Jesus being a better, more qualified judge of a person's actions, words, and motives.

LOVE IS PAINFULLY WONDERFUL

Loving people like God loves us can be painful. It can feel thankless and without reward. However, as we walk in selfless love, we experience a joy and peace that no gratitude or reward could ever give us. When we begin experiencing this joy and peace, our motivation for loving begins to change. We begin to love unconditionally because we desire others to experience the same unconditional love we've experienced from the Heavenly Father.

Recognizing and receiving the perfect love of God will compel us to love others the same way. The Holy Spirit empowers us to live free, life-giving, joy-filled lives.[5] If we lack freedom, life, or joy it is because we've rejected His love in some area of our life — often through our unwillingness to forgive. Without first experiencing the Father's love we lack the experience, motivation, and desire to love those we believe to be undeserving. We are incapable of sharing an experience with others that we have not experienced ourselves.[6]

---

[4] Ephesians 3:14-19; 4:25-5:2; Matthew 18:21-25; Romans 8:31-39; Revelation 5:1-14; See also Sally Lloyd-Jones, and Jago, *The Jesus Storybook Bible: Every Story Whispers His Name.* (ZonderKidz, 2007)
[5] 2 Corinthians 5:16
[6] Matthew 18:21-35; Luke 7:36-50; Ephesians 3:14-19

Years ago, my wife and I ran a college ministry for singles between the ages of 18 and 29. We would meet in a home, eat, have a Bible study, then play some games. Over the years of running this ministry we met in different homes and locations. Most host homes were incredibly generous and hospitable. But I remember one home in particular. It was a very nice home with lots of antique décor, plastic covered couches, and loads of stipulations. We could only eat in the kitchen and use one specified bathroom. While I know the owners were motivated by generosity in their offer to host, it came off as sterile and uninviting. Because we did not feel comfortable there, we ended up moving to a different location within a few weeks.

God fills us with His Spirit to encourage, equip, and empower us to love others. Allowing the Holy Spirit to work through us enables us to partner with Him in His mission. He desires to make His home in our life. However, for Him to be comfortable, we must give Him access to every part of our heart, mind, and life.[7] We must allow Him to search us for areas we may want to keep hidden. We must give Him access to areas we've ignored or forgotten about. It would be very uncomfortable if we invited Him into our lives but then put stipulations on where He could go or where He could sit.

BEING LOVED HELPS YOU LOVE

When we receive God's love, He will put that same love in us for others. Our understanding of how much we've been forgiven will determine the extent to which we forgive others. If we believe we must earn or deserve our forgiveness, we are incapable of extending unconditional forgiveness toward others.[8]

Love is not an emotion or feeling. Love is a choice — a willful

---

[7] John 10:10; 15:1-17; 1 John 4:7-12, 19-21; Ephesians 3:14-19; 4:11-16; Isaiah 61:1-4; Romans 8:9-11; James 4:5-10
[8] Luke 7:36-50; John 17:20-26; Romans 5:5; Matthew 18:21-35

response to people, regardless of their words or actions or whether they reciprocate.[9] Obligated love or conditional love is false love. Loving people out of obligation or condition reveals where we do not fully understand or fully trust the Father's love for us.

His love is patient and kind. It isn't envious or boastful. It is not arrogant. His love does not insist on His own way but is sacrificial. It is not irritable or resentful. It does not rejoice in wrongdoing but rejoices in truth. His love bears all things, has faith in all things, hopes in all things, and endures all things. His love never ends.[10] God loves us because He is love.[11]

If we put limitations or expectations on our love, we are denying people the ability to experience the Father's love. To love others as God loves, we must love unconditionally. This selfless unconditional **love** is *the denial of ourselves — our rights, desires, beliefs, and expectations — for the benefit of others.* Like Jesus, this love prefers others without coercion, compulsion, expectation, manipulation, condition, or requirement. It does not delight in the punishment or negative consequences of those who may deserve it. Rather, it hopes for the best outcome. We love unconditionally because we've been loved unconditionally.

We must allow the Holy Spirit to lead us in how we love each individual person in our lives — regardless of the outcome or perceived receptivity.[12] We cannot judge the effectiveness of our love based upon how others may perceive or receive it. This is especially true when the Holy Spirit leads us to say or do something that could be perceived as harsh or offensive in our love. On

[9] Mark 8:34-38; Luke 6:32-36; 1 John 2:1-11; 3:11-24; 4:7-21; 5:1-5; 1 Corinthians 13:1-13
[10] 1 Corinthians 13:1-13
[11] 1 John 4:7-21
[12] 1 John 4:7-21; Romans 12:14-21

multiple occasions Jesus said and did things that were perceived as offensive. In fact, some people even approached him, confronting him for being offensive.[13]

This means that there are probably times Spirit-led Christians have said or done something that we've perceived as harsh or offensive. We cannot be the judge of what is good, right, and beneficial in love.[14] This also means we cannot judge someone's words or actions as loving or unloving because we cannot see the intentions or motivations of their heart. The measure we use to judge the success of our love (and others) must be the Holy Spirit's peace. We can look at Jesus as our example of how to love because we know that his motivations always had our good in mind.[15]

Ultimately, the Father desires to use us to reveal His love to all people. When we love unconditionally and forgive thoroughly, we are partnering with Him and His mission. As finite beings, we are incapable of showing the infinite love that God is, possesses, and desires to express. This principle is especially true for those who have affected us negatively or people who are repeat offenders in our life.

Loving people on God's terms rather than our own means that we submit to the Father, agree with Jesus for their redemption, and trust the Holy Spirit for our ability to love them purposefully and specifically. We submit to the Holy Spirit by putting His desire for people's freedom above our own desire for revenge or passivity. We agree with Jesus by extending forgiveness as He extended forgiveness toward us — without expectation or requirement. We demonstrate our trust in the Holy Spirit by our willingness to pursue relationship with those who are our enemies — those who have negatively affected us.

---

[13] Matthew 11:6; 15:12, 21-28
[14] Matthew 7:1-5
[15] John 3:16; Romans 5:8; 2 Corinthians 5:18-20

——————— // ———————

Our definition of being worthy of love is often based on acceptable cultural and traditional behaviors we grew up with. Therefore, one's perceived lovability becomes the definition by which we receive and extend love. We live unwilling to forgive when we make one's actions and conduct the prerequisite of our love. Therefore, unconditional standards of love must come from a God who is outside of tradition and culture.

The Gospel is the good news that the Heavenly Father unconditionally loves everyone and has extended unconditional forgiveness toward everyone. God gave everything for us because He loves us and believes we are worth His sacrifice. This sacrificial love is what distinguishes His Kingdom and should be the defining characteristic for all who claim to walk in His Kingdom. However, we may not have been able to recognize and receive His love because of the false definitions of love we've experienced. Therefore, we cannot love like Jesus until we recognize and receive the Heavenly Father's love. When we recognize, receive, and experience His unconditional love, we will forgive thoroughly and love unconditionally.

ACTIVATION STEP

Pray the following prayers. Be sure to take a few moments after you pray to silently wait for the Holy Spirit to respond. Then, write down what He says or shows you.

"Holy Spirit, thank You for loving and caring for my heart and mind. I choose to trust You with the people in my life that have been difficult. Holy Spirit, who are one or two people I find difficult to love and enjoy?

"Holy Spirit, what are some specific things I could say or do to encourage, uplift, or help them?"

Within the next week, do or say the things the Holy Spirit brought to your mind. Be sure to make a note about when, where, and how you will accomplish this task so that you won't forget to do it. You may have to rearrange your schedule for the week to ensure you make time for it.

To further apply this step, ask the Holy Spirit to help you come up with 30 things you can do or say. Then, do one each day for the next 30 days.

CHAPTER TWO

RESET

REVISITING THE RELATIONSHIPS
THAT SHAPED US

Be gentle with one another, sensitive.
Forgive one another as quickly and
thoroughly as God in Christ forgave
you.

— EPHESIANS 4:32, THE MESSAGE

I REMEMBER IT VIVIDLY — THE BLOOD ON THE CEILING AND WALLS.

I had just returned home from spending the weekend in northern Minnesota with my church's youth group. It was incredibly refreshing for me to hang out with friends and leaders who made me feel valued. I was exhausted and energized all at the same time.

As we pulled up to the church, I saw my brother's car waiting to pick me up. This was nothing out of the ordinary since my brother and I were close. As I got in the car, my brother turned to me and told me that mom's boyfriend broke into our house and beat mom's head in with a hammer.

I was numb.

She had already gotten out of the hospital but was staying at a women's shelter. My brother dropped me off at the house for me to unpack before we went to see her. I remember walking into the room where it happened and looking up at the ceiling and walls. Her blood was still there.

I felt nothing.

I was used to violence by this time in my life. I had already seen my dad kick my mom down the stairs. I recall times I saw my dad hit my brother or when he would pick me up by the throat. I had grown accustomed to the threats of him killing me and my mom, or threatening suicide. Or, the time my dad said he had a surprise for my mom and me, then proceeded to drive us out to a graveyard and show us the plots he had pre-purchased. This was just another ordinary horrific circumstance in my life.

My inability to process trauma came to a head during my first year of Bible college. I was having lunch with one of my teachers, sharing stories of my dad, my lack of trust for pastors (since my dad was one), and how I viewed God as some distant punisher rather than a close and caring father. It was about this time when he asked, "Have you forgiven your dad?"

The answer was easy. "Nope!"

This simple conversation led to a mental battle that lasted six months. I remember, nearly every day, coming back to the dorms from the school building tormented by the thought, *You should forgive your dad.* It was a gut-wrenching time filled with emotions I had suppressed for over a decade.

My only thoughts were, *I will never forgive my dad.*

Worn down and nearing the end of the school year, I finally broke. After several hours on my bed, into my tear, snot, and sweat soaked pillow I whispered, "I forgive you." This grew in volume and detail each time I repeated it.

I forgive you for hurting my mom.

I forgive you for making me feel abandoned.

I forgive you for… on and on I went.

After several hours of this, I decided to write my dad a letter. I listed all the things I could remember and closed with, *I love you and I forgive you.*

About a year after writing the letter, I called my dad. I asked him what he thought about it. He replied, "It was good. I disagree because some of that was your mom's fault. But thanks."

This is how I was introduced to real forgiveness.

Forgiveness is an act of the will, regardless of our personal feelings, desires, or beliefs about what we think should happen. It chooses to acknowledge the negative effects or outcomes of a person's behavior on us. Forgiveness then releases our attempts to control those negative effects and outcomes to the Holy Spirit.

Forgiveness releases the offender of any expectations, conditions, or desires we may have of them. The trust we place in the Holy Spirit through forgiveness empowers us to have true, loving compassion and grace for the people who have hurt us. It wasn't until I forgave my dad that I saw how much he loved me, cared for me, and sacrificed for me. Since I was born with Cystic Fibrosis, my dad gave up a secure job, friends and family he loved, and a home he had built to move our family so I could have the best treatment for my disease. His willingness to sacrifice his life for me literally saved my life.

Forgiveness allows our minds to be willing to pursue relationship with the person without requiring something from that relationship. This is not reconciliation, however. **Reconciliation** is *the establishment of peace and harmony back into a relationship through the means of forgiveness and repentance.* Reconciliation of a relationship may not be possible if the other person does not see the need to receive forgiveness or doesn't own their faults. However, through forgiveness we can live free within a relationship even if we aren't reconciled with that person. For a relationship to be fully reconciled, it takes both individuals sacrificially loving and preferring each other.

Restoration of a relationship is the next step after reconciliation. **Restoration** is *the extension of full access and trust to the offending person — enabling a healthy, interdependent relationship.* Restoration requires proven repentance on the part of the offender. **Repentance** is *the act of building new healthy habits and behaviors that are revealed over time.*

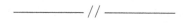

I was addicted to pornography for over 20 years. I struggled with feelings of abandonment and not having value. From these deep-seeded mindsets, I turned to relationships with women and pornography to fulfill my insecurities. As the years went on, the deeper my addiction became.

I hit an all-time low when I was an assistant youth pastor at a church. The stress of my job combined with growing health, financial, and relational issues in my marriage created an unrelenting weight. Added to this, the complete shame, guilt, and hypocrisy I carried as a result of my pornography addiction was overpowering. For a momentary relief, I went to a strip club. This led to me losing my job, moving out of the house we lived in (it was owned by the church for people working in ministry), and all the respect that came with working for a church. I completely broke all trust and security Lacey had in me. This was my lowest point.

We began counseling and working through issues we both had from how we were raised. It was rough. It took a long time. It took sacrificing things that were important to us. I had to learn how to communicate how I was feeling. I had to learn how to deal with my emotions in a healthy way. It wasn't about just stopping my desire to look at porn. It was more about dealing with the underlying thoughts, beliefs, and feelings that came with that addiction. As I was working through these foundational mindsets, I was also working on developing new behaviors that led to new habits. I began to tell Lacey how I felt about stuff. When tempted to go online to look at porn, I would change my surroundings — I would go to the gym or make a sandwich. I had to do something new rather than just stay in the same place and struggle with what I was supposed to do.

It was during this time that we started a production company to produce websites, graphics, and videos for churches and ministries. I had to limit my internet access on both my phone and computer. It can be humiliating having to tell a client that you can't show them their website at a particular time because you currently don't have access to the internet.

We got rid of movies, books, magazines — anything that even hinted at sexual content or could be construed as sexual. It was a rough year. But it was this steadfast determination and building new lifestyles that led to my wife trusting me again.

She had forgiven me immediately when she found out about the strip club. Through owning my faults, we were reconciled. But it wasn't until she saw the changes I was making — my repentance — that our relationship was restored.

Allowing an offending person to have access to your life or extending trust to them is not recommended until repentance has been proven. Healthy boundaries, wisdom, and caution for a season (or the foreseeable future) may be required for safety and security. Restoration may require the advice and wisdom of Spirit-led people you trust and who have your maturity and good in mind.[1]

Reconciliation or restoration may not always be possible because these require the cooperation and participation of the other person. Therefore, distance, death, or simply their unwillingness will lead to the relationship being unreconcilable or unrestored. However, resolution and freedom within the relationship are possible through our willingness to forgive.

GOING BACKWARD TO GO FORWARD

In our pursuit to live in healthy relationships, we must be willing to revisit and resolve past offenses.[2] Forgiving these offenses will empower us to live free of distorted or devalued perceptions of our identity. The quality of our relationships with God and others will greatly improve.[3] The lifestyle of forgiveness

---

[1] A few books we recommend that go deeper into the subject of restoration and boundaries are: *Safe People: How to Find Relationships That are Good for You and Avoid Those That Aren't* (Zondervan, 1996); *Boundaries: When to Say Yes, How to Say No to Take Control of Your Life* (Zondervan, 2017); and *Beyond Boundaries: Learning to Trust Again In Relationships* (Zondervan, 2012). All of these books are written by Dr. John Townsend and Dr. Henry Cloud.
[2] Peter Scazzero, *Emotionally Healthy Spirituality: It's Impossible to be Spiritually Mature, While Remaining Emotionally Immature.* (Thomas Nelson, Inc, 2006), 93-115
[3] Mark 11:25-26; Ephesians 4:31-32

means that we are willing to forgive anything and anyone —
including things we may have forgotten, ignored, or believe we have
already "gotten over."

Our willingness to forgive means we are willing to acknowledge
that people's words and actions have impacted us. This is what the
Bible refers to as "offenses" or "stumbling blocks" (Luke 17:1-2[4]).
This is especially true of people in our developmental and early
growing up years. **Offenses** are *any words or actions that cause emotional,
mental, or physical pain or have caused negative emotions, physical,
circumstantial, or relational effects.*

Due to the daunting and overwhelming nature of some deep,
traumatic, and painful experiences, they can be difficult to forgive.
However, this does not mean that big traumatic offenses are the
only things that negatively affect us. Often, it is the subtle,
seemingly innocuous offenses that do the most damage. These
"insignificant" offenses, if left unresolved, accumulate over time
and grow into unhealthy mindsets and beliefs. Therefore,
regardless of how traumatic or insignificant an offense may be, we
must forgive the offender to be free. This forgiveness will
positively influence our current and future relationships. Resolving
every offense — big or small — through forgiveness leads to
freedom in our mindsets and lifestyles. It will empower us to live
in our God-given identity and walk in our Spirit-led destiny.[5]

——————— // ———————

---

[4] The same Greek word used in Luke 17:1-2 for "temptations to sin" is the same one used
for "offense" or "offended" in Matthew 11:6; 13:57; 15:12; 17:27; Mark 6:3; Luke 7:23; John
6:61; "fall away" in Matthew 13:21; Mark 14:27, 29; John 16:1; and "cause to stumble or sin"
in Matthew 18:6; 24:10; 26:31; Romans 14:21. While this is not an exhaustive list, it points
to the idea that living with unresolved offenses lead us into temptation, sin, and our
relationship with God being negatively affected.
[5] Colossians 3:12-13; Ephesians 4:31-32; Matthew 18:1-35

Our emotional, mental, and often physical reactions in our current relationships are the byproduct of unrelated unresolved offenses, especially in our formative years. These **Formative offenses** are *offenses that happened in our developmental and early growing up years.* They lay the foundation for how we mature, develop, and learn. These offenses influence our reactions to people. If left unaddressed, they form the lenses through which we view every relationship and circumstance. They create a distorted window from which we view our emotions. For example, your current relationships may leave you feeling disrespected, unloved, or rejected (maybe not all the time, but in some instances, those feelings may come up). It is likely that these relationships are not the cause of these feelings. Rather, they are simply pulling on an unresolved emotional thread that began back in your early childhood years. As you go back through your relationships in your growing up years, whether with a teacher, coach, or friend, you may feel the same way: disrespected, unloved, or rejected. These unresolved formative offenses also affect our view of God and how we approach our relationship with Him.[6]

> "Forgiveness does not require the offender to own or admit to any of the offense."

If you have ever played the block game Jenga, you know the strategy is to get the other person to knock over the stack of blocks. Therefore, it would be a waste of time to focus on the top half of the tower — simply managing the most recently played blocks.

---

[6] Luke 17:1-4; Mark 10:13-16. In these passages, Jesus addresses the effects of offense (sins) on young children. His anger is directed toward those who cause — through offense — a child's relationship with God to be hindered. Jesus understands the negative spiritual, physical, and emotional impact that formative offenses have and addresses the need to forgive these people to be free.

This strategy puts us on the defensive and creates unnecessary anxiety and stress for us.

Unfortunately, this is what we do with forgiveness: we usually focus on the people who are most recently affecting our lives. We try to manage our current relationships by living defensive, anxious, and stressed out — hoping not to be the one to mess everything up. A better strategy is to weaken the foundation of these negative patterns by removing blocks closest to the bottom — forgiving offenses where our current unhealthy beliefs began. Removing these foundational offenses (through forgiveness) weakens the lies we believe at their root source. This empowers us to be proactive in our relationships, engaging people in a way that is healthy and life-giving. There are three primary sources of formative offenses.

Formative Relationship #1: Father Figures

Our father is the most influential person in our early growing up years. This includes stepfathers, adoptive fathers, foster fathers, or other father figures in our childhood. However, our biological father plays a uniquely important role by contributing to our genetics, leaving an indelible mark on who we are.

I remember developing journal prompts in ministry school — five questions on a ¼ sheet of paper that I kept in my Bible to help me journal every day. After my dad retired from being a pastor, he gave me his personal library. This library included old Bibles from his time in ministry school. One day, as I was flipping through one of these Bibles, a ¼ sheet of paper dropped out. On it was a list of journal questions nearly identical in layout, subject matter, and phrasing to what I had created. Regardless of whether our relationship with our biological father was healthy, they can influence how we process information and, to a certain degree, how we think, behave, and act.

A father is responsible for protecting us, providing for our needs, and affirming our God-given identity. If our dad is absent or has difficulty meeting these needs (whether purposefully or not), our view of the Heavenly Father being a protector, provider, and identity-giver becomes distorted. Our experience can cause us to polarize our view of His attributes. We either only affirm the attributes we've experienced or completely reject them. For example, if we grew up with an absent, abusive, or a hard-working father, we will either view God as absent, harsh and mean, or only caring about what we can do or produce for Him. We ignore His grace, love, and mercy. Or we will go to the other extreme in viewing Him only as loving, gracious, and compassionate. We reject Him as wrathful, just, and having rules we need to follow.

Because God, the infinite Dad, has chosen to share the title "father" with finite humans (especially our biological fathers), our experience with dad-like figures shapes the lens for how we view God as a dad.

Formative Relationship #2: Mother Figures

Our mother is another significant person in our early growing up years. This also includes stepmothers, adoptive mothers, foster mothers, or other mother figures in our childhood. However, like our biological father, our biological mother plays an important role in our lives by contributing to our genetics. Her mark on us similarly influences how we think and behave. This is especially true throughout the pregnancy. If a mother struggles with substance abuse while pregnant; it can cause issues with emotional regulation, processing delays, and fine-motor developmental issues. Other influences include our mother's thoughts, emotions, and physical actions while pregnant with us.[7] I mention these affects not to criticize or bring fear into those reading this who may be mothers. Rather, I simply want us to acknowledge and affirm the impact our mothers have on us.

A mother is responsible for comforting us, helping and nurturing us, and teaching us. If our mother is absent or seemingly

[7] Laura E. Berk, *Development Through the Lifespan.* (Pearson Education, Inc, 2014, 6th edition), 85-93

too busy to meet our physical, emotional, or mental needs (whether intentionally or not), our view of the Holy Spirit as our comforter, helper, nurturer, and teacher becomes distorted. For example, if we grew up with an absent, emotionally numb, out-of-control, critical, manipulative, or seemingly unhelpful mother, we may view the Holy Spirit as unnecessary, inaccessible, inaudible, impatient, or judgmental. We will tend to ignore His presence, support, and encouragement. Or we will go to the other extreme in seeking Him only for emotional comfort, support, and acceptance — ignoring His conviction, wisdom, and grace.

Because the Holy Spirit has chosen to share His role of comforter, helper, nurturer, and teacher with finite humans (especially our biological moms), our perception of Him is defined by our experiences with these motherly figures.

Formative Relationship #3: Siblings & Peers

Our siblings and peers are the last group of people that significantly influence us in our early growing up years. This includes friends, classmates, and other individuals who are close to us either by their age or common life experience. These people help us learn to communicate and build within us a sense of belonging. When they are able to relate and identify with us, we feel understood and accepted.

I often identify better with people who deal with chronic diseases or ongoing health issues more so than I do with those who are generally healthy. I have also felt understood by elderly folks dealing with the grief of losing their friends. I recall a conversation I had in my twenties with my respiratory therapist; I was asking her about the last few friends I had left from my time growing up in the hospital. She told me they had all died. I felt alone. I often find myself gravitating toward people with similar experiences as me — people who I feel understand me.

If our siblings or peers didn't make us feel important, understood, or accepted growing up, we can develop distorted perceptions of Jesus as a relatable companion,[8] brother, [9] and friend.[10] These negative experiences are compounded by false teachings of Jesus' humanity. They lead us to believe that he can't genuinely identify or sympathize with us.

When Jesus was on earth, he had two natures — divine and human. However, to fully and truly represent, understand, and identify with humanity, he chose to only live out of his human nature. This means that he didn't cling to, take advantage of, or use the privilege of his divine nature as a human; he lived fully trusting and empowered by the Holy Spirit. When we believe that Jesus did what he did by being God, we develop a less-than view of ourselves and our capabilities. We believe that even if we trust the Holy Spirit, we can't actually do what Jesus told us to do; that is, be his disciple and do what he did. Jesus fully understands the struggles that we have in our lives and relationships.[11] He also knows how to overcome those struggles through trusting the Holy Spirit.

Forgiving formative offenses often minimizes, or in some cases, eliminates current offenses altogether. It also guards against similar future offenses. By removing these formative "lenses" through forgiveness, we allow the Holy Spirit to empower us in our

[8] See Hebrews 2:18; 4:15
[9] See Matthew 12:49-50; Romans 8:29
[10] See John 15:15
[11] Philippians 2:5-11. Paul uses the same Greek word for nature, *morphe*. For more on Jesus' humanity see John 1:1-18; Philippians 2:5-11; Colossians 1:15-20; 1 Timothy 2:5-6; Hebrews 2:14-18; 4:15-5:10. Some examples of Jesus' humanity include: he had a human birth and genealogy (Galatians 4:4); he grew and matured in his relationships with God and people (Luke 2:40, 52); he grew in his understanding of obedience (Hebrews 5:8-9); he became hungry and thirsty (Matthew 4:2; John 19:28); he became tired (John 4:6); he had limited knowledge (Mark 13:32); he was mocked, belittled, misunderstood, and betrayed by people close to him (Matthew 13:53-57; Mark 6:1-4; Luke 2:48-51; 4:16-24; 22: 47-48, 63-65; John 6:42; 7:1-5); he grieved the death of loved ones as well as his own death (Matthew 14:10-13a; 26:36-42; Luke 23:46)

relationships. It also brings clarity to our relationship with God and His character — allowing us to experience His broad range of attributes in a more fulfilling way.

REDEFINING FORGIVENESS

God's love for us lead Him to forgive us before we apologize or even think about changing our lifestyles.[12] **Forgiveness** is *the canceling of any past or current actions or responses of a person.* It releases control of how we think a person should act or behave. Forgiveness allows the Holy Spirit to repair or redeem any negative consequences of an offense we may have. These consequences include any negative physical, emotional, or relational effects we are suffering. We must also concede that although we may have dealt with past issues, future consequences may still happen.

I'm going to use a hypothetical situation as an example. A person gets punched in the face — whether by accident or on purpose. On top of the shock, there would be initial pain and some swelling that would take place. If this is all that happened, this encounter might be easy to forgive with its brief consequences. But what happens when the individual wakes up the next morning with a black eye that has swelled shut? There will be a few days of consequences that would need to be forgiven. Or, what happens if the swelling goes down and this person realizes that they still couldn't see? They would have to go to a doctor. Now there are financial consequences that would need to be forgiven. Finally, the doctor examines this person's eye and makes a startling discovery. The impact of the punch caused the optic nerve to separate from the eye, causing permanent blindness. Now, not only is there a future consequence but an ongoing, never ending consequence.

These long-term consequences are often the most difficult consequences to forgive. However, forgiveness chooses to release

---

[12] Matthew 18:21-22; Luke 23:34; Romans 5:8; 2 Corinthians 5:21

control of any future plans we may have had — requiring us to rethink our life's hopes and dreams.

The way Jesus forgave us is the most sacrificial example we can look at. It helps us redefine what we believe about forgiveness and how it was modeled to us in our growing up years. We discover several key characteristics that challenge our perspective and reveal just how incomplete our forgiveness can be.

Characteristic of Jesus' Forgiveness #1:
Forgiving Someone Before They Apologize

Jesus, as he was dying on the cross, desired forgiveness toward those who were killing him.[13] Forgiveness does not require the offender to own or admit to any of the offense. It is freely extended toward the offender regardless of any admission of wrongdoing.

Characteristic of Jesus' Forgiveness #2:
Forgiving Someone Knowing They Won't Stop

Jesus taught us to forgive regardless of how many times someone offended us.[14] Forgiveness is not dependent upon whether the offender ever changes.[15] It is done no matter how many times we are hurt or offended.

Characteristic of Jesus' Forgiveness #3:
Forgiving Pays Someone Else's Debt

When Jesus died on the cross, he suffered the consequences of our hurtful and offending behaviors.[16] Forgiveness is not fair. It pays the price — suffering and enduring the negative consequences — of a wrong we did not commit.

---

[13] Luke 23:34 see also Romans 5:8
[14] Matthew 18:21-35
[15] Keep in mind boundaries may need to be established and full restoration of the relationship may not be possible.
[16] Ephesians 2:1-10; Romans 8:1-11; see also Ezekiel 18:1-32; Jeremiah 31:29-30

———————— // ————————

Choosing forgiveness means we embrace attitudes and mindsets that are often contrary to what we witnessed in our growing up years.[17] The first of these is that we choose to love the person despite their offense. This is a self-sacrificing decision that requires nothing from the person. It releases control of how we believe they should (or should not) behave. This love is demonstrated without preconceived expectations or conditions. Forgiveness resolves an offense by settling it at the extreme conclusion; meaning, we understand that nothing about the person or consequence may ever change. The reality is that this type of love reveals our full trust and dependence on God's kindness toward us. It believes that His love and goodness will be enough to make up for the loss we've experienced.

The second mindset we embrace when choosing to forgive is that we are choosing not to personally punish the person. This means that we do not seek revenge, retribution, or "fairness" in the situation. This is the definition of **mercy**, that is, *withholding from someone deserved penalty or discipline.* This does not mean that authorities are never brought into the circumstance or that negative consequences never happen for the person. Our safety may demand it and civil law may require justice to be served. However, when we forgive, we choose to withhold personal justice — we release bitterness, fault-finding, and grudge-holding from our mind.

This leads to the next choice we embrace when we forgive; that is, releasing negative thoughts and feelings we have toward the person. This is not forgetting. Deeply hurtful and life-changing offenses can rarely be forgotten. In some cases, wisdom requires us to remember and take measures to guard and protect ourselves and others from continuing to be hurt. Rather, not holding a grudge is choosing to keep short accounts with the person,

---

[17] Luke 11:4; 17:3-4; Colossians 3:13; 2 Corinthians 2:6-8

choosing not to bring up past behavior as a weapon. Often, we can tell we're holding a grudge by how we feel. For instance, when the person or situation is brought up, we may still feel hurt or anxious. Forgiveness chooses to look at new offenses as singular events rather than evidence proving the negative beliefs we already have about the person.

Finally, choosing forgiveness chooses to believe the best about the person. This is a hope-filled, Spirit-led response to a person's actions. Forgiveness believes change, redemption, and Spirit-led empowerment are possible for the person. Forgiveness rejects using "always" and "never" statements — choosing to focus on their God-given identity and potential rather than their past or current behavior. This is not ignoring what they've done. It is simply directing our energy and effort toward encouragement, compassion, and supporting them. Ultimately, it trusts that the Holy Spirit can work in the mind and life of the offender.

Forgiveness is neither a feeling nor an automatic reaction. It is an active choice to release an offender of an expectation and entrusting the consequences of their offense to God. While full reconciliation or restoration may not always be possible, real freedom and resolution in our mind and life is always possible through forgiveness. Forgiving past offenses resets how we view people — empowering us to thrive in our relationships the way God designed.

ACTIVATION STEP

Pray the following prayers. Be sure to take a few moments after you pray to silently wait for the Holy Spirit to respond. Then, write down what He says or shows you.

"Holy Spirit, I know You care for me. I trust that You have my best interests in mind. Holy Spirit, who are three people you want me to forgive?"

With the people the Holy Spirit revealed to you, pray the following prayer for each of them.

"Holy Spirit, what have they said or done to me that has negatively affected the way I think or behave?"

Be sure to write down these people along with what the Holy Spirit has revealed to you regarding their negative words or actions toward you. We will revisit these people and offenses in the next chapter.

CHAPTER THREE

BLAME

RETHINKING THE MYTHS
OF FORGIVENESS

"In prayer there is a connection
between what God does and what you
do. You can't get forgiveness from God,
for instance, without also forgiving
others. If you refuse to do your part,
you cut yourself off from God's part."

— MATTHEW 6:14-15, THE MESSAGE

REVENGE WAS THEIR RULE. I WAS JUST HELPING THEM BE TRUE TO THEIR RULE.

Creativity and problem solving are required skills for good parenting. Especially when it comes to discipline. Unfortunately, exhaustion and a sheer lack of will to try can impede these skills. I often find myself muttering, "Just stop, just please, stop!... Just... please..." as I go to my room and shut the door.

I often find myself lacking imaginative ways to ask my girls to stop fighting. One day, I got so fed up I resorted to demanding them take revenge on each other.

A few years back, I had just picked them both up from school and needed to make a quick stop by my office to grab some papers I needed to grade. As I said earlier, I worked at a ministry school where I had developed and taught the Christian Living course. Most of the course was centered around learning how to forgive and resolve conflict.

I could hear my girls screaming at each other inside the car as I left the building. I slowed my pace, regretting my decision to leave my girls by themselves. As I opened my door the accusations began.

"SHE HIT ME!"

"Well, she bit me —"

"Because she touched me."

Both girls were beyond reasoning and had fully embraced brutality as the only means of resolving this conflict. Completely overwhelmed and lacking any self-control myself, I entered the fray.

"Why did you touch her?" I snapped at one of them.

"Because she ripped my art project —"

"She ripped mine first," the other interrupted.

Having my own parental tantrum, I grabbed another art project from my daughters' hands and threw it at her sister. "Here, rip this in half." She looked at me completely stunned. "She ripped yours, rip hers, NOW!"

I had obviously abandoned the conflict resolution techniques I taught in class. She began to cry as she slowly ripped it in half. Once the tear made it through the paper, I grabbed an art project from her bag and threw it at her sister, "Now rip hers. Get even. That *IS* what you want, isn't it?" I sarcastically questioned.

Now, through growing tears and sobs, she muttered, "No, I don't want to be mean. She is my sister. I love her."

After each girl ripped through two more art projects and had become overwhelmingly grief-stricken, the argument was over. I was questioned by my girls for the rest of the drive home.

"Why did you make us ruin each other's projects?"

"Because you wanted revenge so I'm teaching you how to appropriately get revenge on each other. Those are the rules you wanted to live by. I was just helping you two follow those rules."

While I highly discourage you from adding this technique to your personal parenting playbook, I think we are more like my girls then we want to admit. We think that if someone *gets what is coming to them*, the pain from an offense will subside. Reality could not be more different. Our desire for justice and fairness will only intensify the pain we already feel.

We can face many obstacles when presented with the need to forgive. These obstacles are amplified by false definitions of forgiveness. Furthermore, we may have logical reasons as to why forgiveness is not necessary. Our concerns, unanswered questions, or doubts can hinder our willingness to pursue forgiveness. The reality is that our unwillingness to forgive hinders us from being able to feel loved and cared for by God and others. These obstacles, if left unresolved, will eventually lead to us experiencing negative consequences beyond those of the original offense.

This pursuit of freedom, peace, and hope will always be hindered by excuses and confusion.[1] The following are some of the ways we talk ourselves out of needing to forgive.

Excuse #1: "They won't admit they hurt me."

Or, "They won't admit they did anything wrong." The issue is not their lack of repentance. It is our unwillingness to release our expectations and control of what we think should happen (or should not happen). If we do not forgive, we will continue living out of this disappointment. Agreement with the offender can never be the goal. Due to unique perspectives and experiences, two people rarely agree on what is considered offensive. Releasing control and trusting that forgiveness is the best plan moving forward will always lead to emotional freedom and mental peace.[2]

Excuse #2: "They'll just keep doing it."

There will always be people who hurt us — and often in similar ways. However, to live emotionally and mentally free of that pain, we need to forgive. Forgiveness is how we were designed to live whole and healthy lives amidst unhealthy people. This does not mean we have to remain in unhealthy or unsafe relationships. We may have to set up boundaries with wisdom and the advice of Spirit-led people who love us. Building boundaries around these relationships may be healthy and necessary. But for our mind and emotions to be healthy, we must tear down the boundaries of expectations through forgiveness — releasing control of what we want or think should happen.[3]

---

[1] John 10:10; Matthew 7:12; 1 Peter 5:6-10
[2] Colossians 3:13
[3] Matthew 18:21-22; Proverbs 4:14; 24:1-2; 26:11; Psalm 1:1-2

Excuse #3: "They'll get away with it."

This is often accompanied with feeling like they need to suffer the same pain you did. While people may cause us pain — whether emotional, mental, or physical — our unwillingness to forgive can perpetuate this pain. This attitude believes that we are the best judge of fairness and justice. Our desire for revenge hinders our minds from being at peace. Forgiveness chooses to release our control of what we believe should happen to the offender. It allows God the opportunity to fix or redeem what happened to us. The level of freedom and peace we experience in our mind and life is directly affected by our willingness to forgive.[4]

Excuse #4: "I don't want them in my life."

Forgiveness does not equal friendship, reconciliation, or restoration. God does not desire us to live in harmful, unsafe, and abusive circumstances. However, releasing control of our relationships and past experiences to the Holy Spirit, and allowing Him to define the terms of these relationships, will empower us to live free of disappointment and frustration.

Excuse #5: "If I forgive them, then I'm not caring about the other people who got hurt."

This lie prevents us from living as a healthy example to those we love. It hinders us from showing others how to live in peace, wholeness, and freedom. Forgiveness is the deepest and often most painful test of our love; it's how God revealed His love toward us. When we forgive, we are loving those who got hurt by showing them how to live free. While we can be an example of forgiveness, we cannot forgive on someone else's behalf. Their pain is something only they can resolve. We cannot want their freedom more than them; we can only show them the path to that freedom.

---

[4] Romans 12:14-21; Hebrews 10:30; 1 Thessalonians 5:15; 1 Peter 3:9

Excuse #6: "I can't forgive someone who is dead."

Or, "I can't forgive someone I'm no longer in contact with." Both ideas believe reconciliation is a part of forgiveness. As I've previously said, forgiveness is not reuniting a relationship nor is it dependent upon us seeing or speaking to the offender. It does, however, acknowledge the impact the person had on our lives. For us to be healthy in our current relationships, we need to resolve our past relationships.

> "Our unwillingness to talk about past hurts is a symptom of incomplete forgiveness."

THE LIES WE'VE BEEN TAUGHT

When faced with the negative effects of someone's hurtful words or actions, we often choose to diminish, negate, or ignore the need to forgive. In most cases, this is simply how forgiveness was modeled for us in our growing up years. The following thoughts, beliefs, and words are ways we can invalidate the need to forgive or incorrectly apply forgiveness.

Lie #1: "It's okay."

This belief approves of the offense[5] and is most often, the primary way we dismiss other people's hurtful behaviors. This affirming reply comes from our desire to protect ourselves from acknowledging the pain of the offense or the negative effects the person had on us. This can also be an attempt to not offend the other person or avoid conflict with the person who hurt us.

---

[5] See Proverbs 24:23-26

Lie #2: "They did the best they could."

Other forms of this include, *"They had to…"* or *"They didn't know any better."* Admitting that someone failed us does not mean that we lack affection or love for the person. In fact, the ability to understand, identify, or even agree with the offender's behavior or motivation is a gracious response.[6] However, our compassion for them will not diminish or resolve their negative impact on us. While this may be a gracious response, this is not forgiveness. These forms of excusing away the offense inhibits our ability to have peace of mind within the relationship.

Lie #3: "It didn't affect me."

Or, *"They didn't offend me."* Both responses deny the offense and its effects.[7] We are often blind to the impact that people's behaviors had on us. This can come from our desire to not feel hurt by the offense or from appearing weak to the offender. However, the negative effects on our mind have already taken place. In surrounding ourselves with healthy people and allowing them to reveal these blind spots, we are better able to address these issues.

Lie #4: "It's not a big deal."

And, *"It wasn't that bad"* are both forms of diminishing the offense and its effects.[8] While this technically acknowledges that an offense took place, it minimizes the full extent of its effects or influence. It is impossible to fully forgive if we do not acknowledge the full weight of an offense. We will continue to live under negative attitudes, thoughts, beliefs, and feelings when we belittle their origin.

---

[6] See Proverbs 18:21
[7] See Proverbs 18:1; 26:24-26
[8] See Proverbs 18:5

Lie #5: "Forgive and forget."

The Christian form of this is, *"Jesus wouldn't want me to dwell on it anymore,"* or *"It's under the blood and doesn't affect me anymore."* These false views negate the impact an offense has on us[9] and Jesus' commands to forgive.[10] This approach believes that if we don't think or talk about an experience then we won't suffer from its effects. Ignoring or forgetting an offense does not resolve it. We often resort to this definition of forgiveness when an experience brings up painful emotions and anxiety when we talk about it.

As Christians, we can wrongly believe that the *"past is the past"* and that dwelling on the past is a selfish focus on ourselves rather than God. However, this unwillingness to talk about our past is a signal of incomplete forgiveness. We mistakenly believe that focusing on what brings us joy and "being blessed" resolves our issues. This couldn't be further from the truth. While we shouldn't gossip, slander, malign, or talk bad about people,[11] the pain and ongoing negative effects of other's behavior on us may still be affecting us. Moreover, it is when we forgive and are free of the emotional pain and anxiety of an offense, we can offer real help to others by sharing our story. We bring hope to those who are struggling when we share our experience with them. This is true evangelism.[12]

One final note is that deep, life-changing offenses are often impossible to forget. "Forgetting" an offense while continuing to be in close proximity with the person who hurt us can be unwise and lead to further pain and trauma. For our safety and protection, we may need to remember offenses while still demonstrating forgiveness and relational boundaries.

---

[9] See Proverbs 26:11; 22:24
[10] Matthew 6:14-15; Luke 17:3-4
[11] See Colossians 3:8-13
[12] See Revelation 12:11

Lie #6: "I will never reconcile with ____."

Or, *"I can't reconcile with ____."* Forgiveness is often wrongly used as a synonym for reconciliation. Since we have already covered this at length in the previous chapter, I will simply say that reconciliation requires both people to participate; one extending forgiveness and the other receiving it and living out proven repentance.

Lie #7: "I won't allow ____ back into my life."

As I've stated before, forgiveness is not the restoration of a relationship. Trust, the catalyst to restoration, is gained slowly over time through a season of the person proving new behaviors. Scripture is clear that God alone is who we are to trust unconditionally.[13] Therefore, reconciliation and restoration of a relationship with people may not always be possible. However, peace of mind and emotional freedom from an offender is always possible through forgiveness.

NEGATIVE EFFECT OF NOT FORGIVING

Refusing, neglecting, or wrongly defining forgiveness produces negative effects in our mind and life,[14] which compound the negative effects we may already be suffering as a result of the original offense. As you'll see, they progressively get worse as we continue to refuse forgiveness.

Negative Effect #1: Heaviness

This mental, emotional, and spiritual weight can feel very physical. This heaviness is caused by the conviction of our conscience and the Holy Spirit. It is the signal that something in our thinking or behavior is in opposition to how we were designed

---

[13] See Jeremiah 17:5-8; 2 Chronicles 32:8; Psalm 118:8-9; 146:3; Romans 1:24-25
[14] Isaiah 57:20-21; 59:1-2; Psalm 32:1-4; Proverbs 28:13-14; Matthew 6:14-15; Luke 6:36-45; 2 Corinthians 2:6-11

to live. While it may feel painful, guilt is a symptom that something is wrong. If we ignore this symptom, our thoughts and behavior can take a tragic turn.

Negative Effect #2: Torment

This self-inflicted agony results from continuing to believe lies about ourselves, God, and others. Torment often comes as a voice in our head that devalues our identity. This distorted perception of ourselves inhibits what we think we can do. It negatively affects our reactions and behaviors. We either believe we are powerless or feel like we must try harder and do better. Torment is ultimately the result of us separating ourselves from God through our willful choice to not resolve an offense. Our prayers become hindered and our relationships suffer. We feel out of control, hopeless, anxious, and restless. However, the Father's kindness will always pursue and reveal areas in our mind and lives where we are living less-than our intended design and destiny.

Negative Effect #3: Frustration & Disappointment

Unresolved issues will always leave us feeling edgy and irritated. When we entrust these feelings to the Holy Spirit and genuinely examine them, they can point us to the real issue. Left unaddressed, we develop reactions out of these issues that destroy our relationships and affect our mental and emotional health.

Negative Effect #4: Bitterness & Anger

These reactions to people result from unhealthy or negative emotions. While the emotions that trigger anger (an external reaction) and bitterness (an internal reaction) will vary from person to person, the result is the same. Both reactions can cause the numbness and death of emotions and relationships. We amplify our own suffering as well as the tension within a relationship when we react to people with bitterness or anger.

Negative Effect #5: Destructive Habits & Behaviors

Unhealthy habits and behaviors emanate out of our unresolved offenses. These may even be behaviors that seem normal or natural to us. This is especially true of offenses received in our developmental and early growing up years. We react in our relationships (especially to difficult people) from this underlying pain and disappointment. Ultimately, we hurt others while continuing to hurt ourselves.

There will always be reasons, excuses, and hindrances to pursuing forgiveness and freedom. Some of these may be logical, convenient, and justifiable. You may even have people in your life defending these reasons — agreeing with your unwillingness to forgive. Additionally, our own false or misguided definitions of forgiveness further prevent us from experiencing freedom and peace. God desires good for us — He wants us to live free of pain and anxiety within relationships.

If there is even a hint of doubt, pain, or aversion to an offense or person, we should revisit forgiveness. Reexamining our motives and apprehension to forgiveness invites the Holy Spirit to bring clarity to our mind. Even if we feel we have already fully forgiven, our willingness to revisit the person or offense will only bring deeper freedom and peace. Make the person or offense a non-issue in your life and mind.

ACTIVATION STEP

Forgiveness can be difficult, confusing, and overwhelming. It can take time and require us to revisit painful memories we would like to just as soon forget. My goal in discussing forgiveness is to lead you to freedom, not heartache.

Therefore, to help bring clarity and resolution to your mind, we've developed a practical step-by-step process to forgiveness called *The Freedom Booklet* that we've included in the back of this book. Use it to resolve the offenses the Holy Spirit brought to your attention at the end of chapter two. I encourage you to take this time, while it is fresh in your mind, to revisit these offenses — allowing the Holy Spirit to care for those painful memories and circumstances. Be sure to complete the steps for each person He revealed, one at a time. Remember, the Holy Spirit brought them up for a reason. He wants to heal these areas in your mind. Don't allow this opportunity to pass — He is faithful and will give you freedom, hope, and peace as you forgive these people and entrust these offenses to the Holy Spirit.

I fully understand that you may not be ready to take this step; I would hate for you to feel stuck here. Please feel free to go on to the next chapter but be mindful that your wholeness may only come out of your willingness to forgive and release control to God.

Whatever you choose, I truly believe the Holy Spirit will give you clarity and hope as you continue through this book — He will speak life and encouragement to your soul. Let's close this chapter by praying the following prayer.

"Heavenly Father, thank You for loving me and caring for me. I trust that You have good for me. Jesus, I know that you understand my struggle to forgive but that you also desire my freedom. Holy Spirit, I ask that You bring hope and peace to my mind as I move forward. I trust Your faithfulness."

CHAPTER FOUR

GROSS

REJECTING SHAME
AND RESOLVING GUILT

So now, those who are in Christ Jesus
are not judged guilty.

— ROMANS 5:6-8, THE MESSAGE

THE ICE CREAM BECAME DISGUSTING — IT WAS THE PRODUCT OF A LIE.

When my wife was growing up, her family lived in a neighborhood filled with children and family-friendly block parties. In this idyllic community sat a library a few blocks from her house. Lacey loved reading and would often visit this library. She also liked ice cream. Unfortunately, her favorite ice cream shop sat outside her neighborhood in an unsafe part of the city. One afternoon she asked her mom if she could go to the library but once she left the house, she immediately headed to the ice cream shop.

"I went to Millers (the name of the ice cream shop) because it was the best and they gave you the most; three scoops for a dollar," she recalls as she tells me the story.

Looking at all the flavors, she zeroed in on her favorite, mint chocolate chip. Giving the cashier the money, she accepted her minty treat. Stepping away from the counter, she took her first lick.

What have I done?, she thought.

Shame and guilt began to flood her mind. Rather than being refreshed by the cone she became repulsed. The chocolate-mint flavor became gross to her. She had betrayed her mom's trust; now the lie manifested in cone she held melting in her hand. She immediately threw the cone in the trash and ran home.

Lacey confessed the lie to her mom, telling her how she had gone to the ice cream shop instead of the library. She apologized for breaking her mom's trust and received her mom's forgiveness.

Lacey still loves ice cream. She has not let this situation determine her view of ice cream — looking at it in disgust or regret. She embraces it for the refreshing treat that it is because she was able to fully embrace being forgiven.

——————— // ———————

God has forgiven every person who ever lived. This forgiveness is thorough and complete.[1] The process of reconciliation with Him begins when we receive this forgiveness — trusting Him to not hold our misdeeds against us.[2]

Reconciliation with God consists of both receiving His forgiveness and building new mindsets and behaviors. Receiving forgiveness results in us no longer being condemned for our unhealthy mindsets and behaviors.[3] We are free from the negative mindsets we have as a result of breaking our relationship with Him and others. It is as if our unhealthy and unnatural actions and thoughts never existed.[4]

Because of our memories, we can be tempted to focus on our sins, failures, and mistakes. We develop a false perception of our identities because of the thoughts and actions we've taken. This identity is filled with shame, guilt, regret, and self-deprecation. However, when we trust that God has truly and thoroughly resolved our destructive mindsets and behaviors, we will live in peace, joy, and contentment.

The reality is that the Holy Spirit is more powerful than anything we have ever done. He can fix or redeem the mean, harmful, or unhealthy things we've done to people. Releasing control and allowing Him to work in us sets us free from regret.

FALSE VIEWS OF GOD'S RESPONSE TO US

We learn and develop false views of forgiveness, redemption, love, and acceptance based on the experiences in our early childhood years. We create personal "laws" from these mindsets that define our relationships. We expect people to behave by these laws — making our love and acceptance of them conditional to the

---

[1] John 3:16-21; 19:30. See also Proverbs 18:3; 1 John 2:2; 4:13-18; Romans 5:8, 18; 8:12-17
[2] Romans 5:11. See also 2 Corinthians 5:18-19
[3] Romans 8:1
[4] 2 Corinthians 7:10

way they behave. Scripture refers to this law-making process as hardening or enslaving our heart and mind (also, "walking after the flesh").[5] **The Gospel** is simply *the message of how God has responded to our attitudes, thoughts, and behaviors that hurt or hinder our relationship with Him.* When we define the Gospel by our experience, we develop false beliefs about how God responds to us.

False Belief #1: Performance-Based Love & Value

Whether it's friendships, dating, or marriage, I've heard people say that they will only be friends with _____, date _____, or marry _____ if they _____. They then list their terms for the person and relationship. Rather than focusing on what they like about the person, they make the relationship all about the behaviors they expect from them.

This mindset believes that people are only loveable or valuable based upon what they do or how they act. The lie is that someone's worthiness to be loved and valued is synonymous with, or dependent upon, how well they meet our expectations. This approach to relationships is often the by-product of excessive unhelpful criticism in our growing up years. It can also result from inflexible adherence to a set of family, cultural, or religious rules and regulations being demanded of us.

This lie opposes the truth of the Gospel that God created and loves every single person who has ever lived. It denies the reality that our worth and value are given to us by God and therefore cannot be earned or taken away. It is God's character rather than our behavior that determines our identity.[6]

---

[5] "Harden" – Deuteronomy 15:7; Proverbs 28:14; 2 Corinthians 3:14; Hebrews 3:8, 13; "Slavery" – John 8:34; Romans 8:16; 2 Peter 2:19; "Walking after the flesh" – Romans 8:4; Colossians 3:7; Galatians 5:16-26: Ephesians 2:1-2; 4:17. It should be noted that the same Greek word for "flesh", *sarx*, used in Galatians 5 is also used in reference to Jesus in John 1:14. Therefore, the idea of walking after the flesh does not mean our flesh is inherently sinful; rather, it means that when we trust and fulfill the needs and desires of our flesh outside of trusting God, we will develop unhealthy, habitually inclined, sinful habits and behaviors. See also Jeremiah 17:5-8.

[6] Genesis 1:27; Psalm 107:1; John 3:16; Ephesians 3:14-19; Romans 5:8; 8:38-39; 1 John 4:7-16. See also Genesis 9:6; James 3:9; Ephesians 3:14-15

False Belief #2: Conditional Forgiveness

This mindset believes that people should only be forgiven or redeemed if their actions and effort earn or merit it. The lie in this belief is that mistakes and failures will be cancelled only when the other person purposefully suffers for them or works hard enough to outweigh them. This is often a by-product of wrongly defined forgiveness and redemption demonstrated to us.

> ## "It is God's character rather than our behavior that determines our identity."

I've often seen people's commitment to a relationship — whether friend, dating, or marriage — be based upon what the other person should be doing. This is often stated, "I will only stay friends with _____, continue dating _____, or stay married to _____ if they…" Basically, they are only agreeing to stay in the relationship if the other person changes or meets their demands.

This lie opposes the truth of how God has forgiven us. He has already extended forgiveness to every person.[7] All we do is simply choose to believe He forgave us and receive it.[8] Furthermore, our redemption is not based upon our ability to live morally.

THE LENSES WE VIEW LIFE THROUGH

A few years back, Lacey was talking with a woman going through a divorce. The woman revealed that she hadn't trusted her husband throughout their entire marriage; so, when her husband had an affair, she felt justified. Over the course of the discussion

---

[7] See Matthew 26:27; Ephesians 4:32
[8] Acts 10:43; Romans 3:24; Ephesians 1:7; Colossians 1:14

Lacey found out that this woman's trust issues with men led back
to an experience she had with her dad. This formative experience
became the lens through which this woman viewed the men in her
life — sabotaging every relationship she had. It wasn't until she
was willing to forgive her dad that she recognized this "lens" as a
major contributing factor to the failure of her marriage.

We develop "lenses" from our experiences that shape our
perspective of current situations. For example, an Olympic
swimmer will view a body of water differently than someone whose
child drowned. The body of water didn't change. It was their
experience with water that formed their perspective. Similarly, we
interpret life and relationships through the lenses we've developed.

Our View of Ourselves

A distorted and devalued perception of our identity is
developed through what is said and done to us in our growing up
years. We form beliefs about forgiveness and love based on how
people respond to our mistakes and failures — believing we must
earn or prove our worth. From these beliefs we develop
performance-based behaviors. This leads to attitudes of fear,
shame, and regret.

We strengthen this hopeless perspective by ignoring, denying,
or rejecting God's love, mercy, forgiveness, and grace. This
demeaning view of our identity is further re-enforced through
degrading Christian doctrines we may have been taught. These
hopeless attitudes become seemingly inseparable from our identity
and become a catalyst for our behavior. Who we believe we are will
influence what we do. Our identity (or the wrong perception of it)
will determine how we behave.

Our View of Others

The distorted or devalued perception of our own identity
causes us to negatively interpret people's words and actions. We
believe the worst and therefore develop condemning assumptions

about their behavior. When we react to them from these assumptions, we distort and devalue how they view their identity. Essentially, our distorted lens of them contribute to their distorted lens of themselves.

Our condemning assumptions and unwillingness to forgive perpetuate their feelings of fear, shame, and regret. Living with condemning assumptions negates how the Holy Spirit may be working in their mind and life. Ultimately, we deny them safety, peace, and the space to grow. Our response to them will either hinder or help them experience God's grace, love, and freedom.

Our View of God

Finally, having a distorted and devalued perception of our own identity causes us to believe God is someone to hide from when we make a mistake or fail (Genesis 3:8-10). We view Him as distant and withdrawn. When we wrongly assume God's forgiveness and redemption are based upon our ability to earn or prove our worth, we are wrongly believing we must behave correctly to be loved by Him. We develop performance-based habits that affirm our belief that God demands certain behaviors from us to be in right relationship with Him.

Building habits that are focused on our mistakes and failures lead us to believe that the Heavenly Father focuses on those as well. With this mindset, our relationship with Him is built upon fear, shame, and regret rather than love, confidence, and empowerment. We live void of God's hope and peace when we don't believe He loves and forgives unconditionally. In believing a lie about His character, we reject His love and forgiveness. We believe, as we do with other people, that His love and acceptance of us are only based upon how we behave.

———— // ————

God has forgiven us of all our sins, failures, and mistakes. There is nothing we need to do to achieve His forgiveness.[9] We are freed from shame and condemnation when we repent and trust His faithfulness rather than our performance.

God is always pursuing relationship with us — with everyone.[10] In His pursuit, He will encourage us to walk in step with His Spirit, building life-giving attitudes, thoughts, and beliefs of ourselves, others, and Him. Trusting that God is good and that His character and desire for us is good enables us to hear what the Holy Spirit is already speaking to our mind and heart. We expose the lies we're believing by giving Him access and permission into the dark areas of our heart and mind.[11] Confessing these lies is the first step to living the free and whole life God created you to live.[12]

There will be people and circumstances in our lives that remind us of our failures and mistakes. Furthermore, there is a spiritual enemy who wants to destroy our mind and relationships.[13] Thankfully, God, in His kindness, will reveal unresolved mindsets and behaviors that hurt ourselves and others. This conviction will be hope-filled and specific.[14] It will lead to freedom and peace rather than shame and regret.

Paul writes to a church in Corinth that this conviction, if allowed to have its full effect, leads to freedom and restoration through healthy sorrow and life-changing mindsets and behaviors (2 Corinthians 7:10). Real guilt comes from the conviction of a grace-filled God who desires us to live free of real failure. Releasing these failures leads to real hope-filled life-changing mindsets and behaviors. This is what Scripture refers to as walking after the Spirit

---

[9] Hosea 6:6; Micah 6:6-8; 2 Corinthians 5:16-21; Romans 2:1-5; 5:12-21; 10:5-13; 1 Peter 2:6; 1 John 1:7-10; 2:1-2
[10] Isaiah 65:2; John 12:32
[11] John 3:19-21
[12] Acts 19:18; 1 John 1:9
[13] Revelation 12:10-11; John 10:10
[14] Romans 2:4; John 16:7-15

rather than "the flesh" (unnatural behaviors and cravings).[15] We are continually encouraged to repent — move from trusting ourselves to trusting God; this is how we no longer walk after "the flesh."

When we walk after the Spirit — how God designed us to live — we no longer give into the unnatural desires to which we have habitually inclined or enslaved ourselves. Our repentance joined with His forgiveness frees us from guilt, condemnation, shame, and regret. It releases our failures into the Father's control and receives grace from the Holy Spirit to change.

Our definitions of love and value are based upon acceptable cultural behaviors we learned as children. These experiences lead us to believe that our lovability and value come from our effort or achievements. Therefore, unconditional standards of love and value must come from a God who is outside of every culture. This is the point of the Gospel — the encouraging message that God unconditionally loves and has extended unconditional forgiveness toward everyone. God gave everything for us because He loves us and believes we are worth His sacrifice.

God has always extended His love toward us. However, we may not have recognized or received this love because of our own unresolved pasts. We will not be able to feel loved by Him until we replace our false definitions of love and forgiveness. We will not be able to love and forgive others until we accept and receive His love and forgiveness.

Our repentance to the Holy Spirit's conviction empowers us to develop and cultivate new, life-giving mindsets and behaviors. These Spirit-led responses and healthy coping behaviors realign us to God's original design and destiny for our lives.

---

[15] John 8:34; Romans 6:6, 13; 8:16-20; 2 Peter 2:18; Colossians 3:1-10; Ephesians 4:22, 24; Galatians 5:1, 16-17

ACTIVATION STEP

Pray the following prayers. Be sure to take a few moments after you pray to silently wait for the Holy Spirit to respond. Then, write down what He says or shows you.

"Holy Spirit, thank you for loving me despite whatever mistrust or distrust I may have toward You. I will choose to trust that You desire good for me. Holy Spirit, who is someone that is difficult for me to see separate from their hurtful words, lifestyles, or behaviors?"

"Holy Spirit, what are some encouraging and uplifting words and thoughts that You want me to have for this person?"

Write these words and thoughts down into a note or letter. Send or give this note to the person within the next week. If you live with them, you could place the note in a place you know they will find it — by a mirror, on a coffee maker, etc. Challenge yourself to only believe and say positive things by avoiding questions, accusations, or bringing up unmet expectations.

It may be worth noting that the person the Holy Spirit brought to your mind may be unsafe or unwise for you to approach. While I do not recommend you reconnect with this person, I still suggest you follow the prompts and write down what the Holy Spirit said to you.

CHAPTER FIVE

HARSH

LEARNING TO ACCEPT
PAINFUL HELP

But I tell you the truth, it is better for you that I go away. When I go away, I will send the Helper to you. If I do not go away, the Helper will not come.

— JOHN 17:7, THE MESSAGE

IT WAS CLEAR TO ME THAT MY WIFE OBVIOUSLY DIDN'T HEAR GOD'S VOICE.

I was born to start a church… or so I thought.

Our family had just returned from a 6-month mission trip in Ireland when I discovered this was what God was directing me toward. This was my purpose.

Living with a terminal disease (in my case, Cystic Fibrosis) places an urgency on fulfilling goals you've set. At the age of twenty-eight, I was nearing a mid-life crisis of sorts. I never envisioned myself living past thirty, so I was quickly nearing the last benchmark I had set for myself. Additionally, one particularly successful pastor I followed was twenty-five when he started his church. I already felt behind.

The week we arrived back from Ireland I had scheduled for my wife and me to attend a conference on how to start a church. I had spent the last 6 months developing a 15-page business plan — detailing the ministry model and philosophy along with the location and demographic our church would reach. I was all ready to move forward; I just needed to finish this conference, get their endorsement, then I would be on my way.

This three-day conference was amazing. We learned so much about everything it would take to start a new church. There were charts, graphs, and incredibly talented speakers who had successfully started churches themselves. I was beyond motivated and encouraged.

The final session was a Q&A with these pastors. The questions people were asking focused on things I had already figured out.

Where should I start a church? What model is the most successful? Who should I invite to be a part of my launch team?

These were easy questions. I had already answered them all in my business plan.

Then it happened.

My wife raised her hand.

We had talked openly about my vision to start a church. We discussed our concerns. We had talked through — and in my opinion, agreed upon — the necessary issues and next steps we would need to take. So when I saw her hand go up, I thought she was going to ask the wives about their role and how to best support their husbands in starting a new church.

"How do you support your husband in starting a church —" her voice broke. Tears began streaming down her face. "— when you, as the wife, don't feel called to start a church?"

I was both dumbfounded and crushed.

We had already talked about this. We had already dealt with her concerns. In my mind, I began questioning her ability to hear from God. *Why was she asking this? She's ruining everything.*

The pastor looked me squarely in the eyes and said, "If your wife isn't behind your desire to start a church, you will fail. And I would question whether you've actually heard from God. You're first priority is to care for your wife. And you're obviously not doing that if she's not behind you."

I was devastated and mortified all at the same time.

"I would like to talk with you both after the conference. I think there are a lot of things you —" he looked at me in contempt, "— need to realize."

After they closed the Q&A session down, the main speaker met us at our table. He laid out how I was failing at my primary responsibility as a husband. I was not caring for my wife. He sympathized with Lacey and told her that God would not allow me to succeed if she wasn't on board.

This pastor did not pull any punches. He was brutally honest with me. It was one of the harshest, most mortifying conversations I have been a part of. I was completely crushed.

The 6-hour drive home was rough.

We talked through the pastor's words. I got angry. Lacey cried a lot. Then there were long stretches of silence.

In the days that followed the conference, I began to realize that his words were the best advice I would receive. The reality was, I did not have the abilities or personality to start a new church. I literally lacked in every area that a successful, caring, charismatic person would need to start a new church.

The pastor was mean. But he wasn't wrong. His harshness was only out of a love for my wife and me. It was his harshness that led me to question and re-evaluate my abilities and purpose. It was his harshness that halted my stubborn pursuit toward failure. Ultimately, his harshness united my wife and me in pursuit of what would eventually become Cultivate.

Conviction will often come through imperfect people who do so imperfectly. But the Holy Spirit's conviction will always be specific, thorough, life-giving, and hope-filled even if it doesn't feel that way in the moment. His conviction is not about telling us what we're doing wrong, even if that's what it feels like. He is more concerned about us doing what He designed us to do. He reveals areas in our mind and life that are not in alignment with how He created us — things that are stealing, killing, and destroying us.

Unfortunately, we've trained ourselves to become offended when criticism comes. We try to defend or justify our thoughts and behaviors. This usually comes from feeling like we need to guard or fight against feeling pain and discomfort. Our spiritual enemy tries to further this pain and discomfort by condemning us through vague, incomplete or inaccurate accusations. These accusations will leave us feeling hopeless and anxious.

Our repentance — changing our mind and behaviors — reveals our trust in God's love, grace, and mercy. This trust produces a joy void of regret and shame.[1] This joy comes from knowing and receiving the Father's forgiveness — recognizing that He no longer holds our unhealthy mindsets and behaviors against us. Beyond this, our repentance reveals our belief that God is bigger and more powerful than any negative consequences our thoughts and actions have caused. In receiving God's forgiveness, we are releasing and entrusting to Him the people we've hurt.

> "Our repentance to the Father does not earn us His forgiveness; rather, our repentance is our response to His forgiveness."

SIN, RIGHTEOUSNESS, & JUDGEMENT

Jesus told his disciples in John 16 that it was vital that he leave so that the Helper could come (John 16:7-11). This Helper would bring a conviction that would lead us to life-giving, hope-filled thoughts and behaviors. **Conviction** is *the voice of the Holy Spirit, through our conscience, that encourages us to think and behave how we were designed to by God.* This conviction can come through our thoughts, people, and the Scriptures.

God created us with a conscience. As children, we are sensitive to our conscience — the area in our mind that is in harmony with the Holy Spirit's voice. This conscience is like a radio. Radio waves are always around us carrying thousands of music, news, and talk show stations. However, if the volume is turned down on our radios, we will not be able to hear those stations. The same is true of our conscience — the radio tuned into the Holy Spirit's radio

---

[1] See 2 Corinthians 7:10; Nehemiah 8:1-18; 2 Samuel 12:23

station. As we choose to ignore His voice, we silence it to the point of becoming seemingly non-existent. Soon, attitudes, thoughts, and behaviors that once bothered us — those that are unhealthy and unnatural to our design — become normal, natural, and right.[2] We become deaf to the Spirit's voice.

God is always talking. Like different radios being in different rooms of our house this can also be true of different areas of our lives. In one area of our life, like finances or a specific relationship, we can hear the Holy Spirit's voice clearly. It's vibrant, encouraging, and life-giving. However, in another area ("room") in our life, we may have His voice turned down. There may be a specific relationship or circumstance that we do not want to know God's thoughts. Unfortunately, because of the areas we can hear His voice, we believe our relationship with Him and others is healthy. However, the reality is that we are becoming stagnate, slowly becoming unresponsive to His voice. Over time, this will affect every area of our life — even the areas we view as healthy and vibrant.

At the core of our design is the need to be in relationship with the Holy Spirit. This trusting — our love and submission to Him — is greater and preeminent above the people we love (e.g., family, friends, spouse, children, etc.).[3] The Holy Spirit will convict us whenever we've broken relationship with someone through willful sin or unintentional mistakes or failures. For example, when I was addicted to pornography, this was an obvious and constant area He would convict me. Also, when I would promise my wife that I would take out the trash and forget, or intentionally left it behind, He would also convict me of this. Both of these led to broken relationship with my wife.

He will convict us of wrong motivations despite being justified or right in our actions and words. I remember one fight my wife and I had when I literally said nothing. After about ten minutes of

---

[2] See Proverbs 14:12; 16:25
[3] See Luke 14:25-26; Romans 1:18-32

her berating me amidst my silence, she stomped out of the room and made her way to our bedroom. I hadn't said anything wrong. In fact, I don't even think I actually did anything wrong to prompt this rebuke. But after about ten more minutes sitting on the couch wondering what I had done (and justifying myself in my silence) I was deeply convicted for hurting my wife's feelings. I realized that it was my silence and unresponsiveness that was escalating the conversation. I knew I had to apologize to her for not caring for her feelings. According to John 16, the Holy Spirit will convict us for sin, righteousness, and judgment.

Holy Spirit Convicts Us of Sin

The Scriptures generally use the terms sin, unrighteousness, and ungodliness interchangeably.[4] However, based upon John 16:8-10, Romans 1:18; and 14:23, we can define these terms in the following ways: **Unrighteousness** is *any thought or behavior that disagrees with God and His design for how we are to fulfill our God-given needs and desires.* These are any of our beliefs, words, or actions in direct opposition to God and His desires for us. **Self-righteousness** is *any thought or behavior that does not acknowledge God and His design for how we are to fulfill our God-given needs and desires.* These are any of our beliefs, words, or actions that do not credit God as the ultimate source of empowerment. While we may have righteous behaviors — things we do that are in line with God's design and desire for us — our motivations may not always affirm God's presence or involvement. Therefore, while our actions may be righteous, our motivation is ungodly. **Ungodliness** is *any mistrust or distrust we have of God.* It is often revealed in our self-righteousness, self-reliance, and self-determination.[5]

Our sin will involve either or both unrighteousness and ungodliness. Therefore, we can define **Sin** as *the broad description of our intentional or unintentional distrust or mistrust of God in our thoughts and*

---

[4] See John 16:8-10; Romans 1:18, 14:23; 1 Timothy 1:9; 1 Peter 4:18; Jude 14-18
[5] See Deuteronomy 8:5-20

behaviors.[6] It is our lack of faith in God or our unwillingness to bring Him glory.[7] This results in thoughts and behaviors that are unrighteous, self-righteous, and ungodly.

With all these different and often confusing elements to sin, the Holy Spirit's conviction will be thorough. Going deeper than just encouraging changed behavior, He will reveal the underlying lie that forms the basis our sinful thoughts and behaviors. He will bring truth to our minds to help us overpower the lies we believe about having a sinful identity and our inability to not sin. Ultimately, He desires us to experience His love, goodness, and provision so we are no longer led by our mistrust or distrust.

Holy Spirit Convicts Us of Righteousness

Healthy lifestyles will strengthen and affirm how God created us physically, emotionally, mentally, and relationally. **Righteousness** therefore is *any attitude, action, or behavior that agrees with God and how He designed us to fulfill our God-given needs and desires.*[8] The Spirit's conviction of righteousness happens because Jesus is no longer with us as a physical human representation of how to live.

The Holy Spirit is our personal helper, not a generic law enforcer. He reveals what to believe and how to behave in each unique relationship. His guidance leads us into healthy, life-giving, and hope-filled mindsets and behaviors. This is a positive form of conviction. It is the assurance or confidence of knowing how to think and behave.

Holy Spirit Convicts Us of Judgement

The most powerful weapon we have against our spiritual enemy is the conviction of his judgement — the revelation of his defeat. Jesus disarmed and condemned the enemy when he lived his life

---

[6] See Deuteronomy 8:11-20; Romans 14:23; Galatians 2:16; 1 John 3:23
[7] See Romans 1:17; 14:23; Hebrews 11:6; 1 Corinthians 10:31; Galatians 3:11; Colossians 3:17, 23
[8] See Acts 17:31; Romans 6:13; 8:5; Philippians 3:9; 1 Timothy 6:11

empowered by the Holy Spirit, trusting the Father's plan.[9] Jesus took back humanity's authority over creation when he judged, condemned, and defeated the enemy.

Although Jesus won the war against the enemy, we take part in seeing this realized in our life. We can surrender back to the enemy the personal victory, power, and authority Jesus won for us. First Peter 5:8 describes the enemy as prowling around *like* a roaring lion, seeking someone to destroy. Prowling lions do not roar — they would scare off their prey. Therefore, Peter is saying that the only weapon our enemy has is his voice (the ability to lie and deceive us).

The enemy captures ground in our minds when we believe his lies about our identity. We agree with him when we believe: 1) our identity is distorted and devalued rather than intrinsic; 2) our identity is earned rather than received; and 3) our identity is lost or gained rather than freely given by God. When we submit to these lies about our identity, our activity follows. If we believe a less-than truth about our identity (for example, that we are merely sinners saved by grace), we will approach temptation timidly and often give in without a fight. However, the Scriptures say we are more than conquerors.[10] Believing our identity and ability are designed for victory empowers us to face every relationship with hope and clarity.

It is important we allow the Holy Spirit to empower us to discern and be aware of the enemy's scheme. Ignoring, denying, or concealing these lies and temptations only empowers them in our mind and life. Amidst these lies, the Holy Spirit convicts us of disagreeing with God's judgement of the enemy and reminds us of the enemy's defeat. As His creation, He warns us against participating with a defeated team. He convicts us toward living how He designed us to; that is, in victory and freedom.

---

[9] See Colossians 2:8-15; John 12:30-32. See also John 9:39; Luke 10:17-20; Hebrews 2:14-18; 1 John 3:8; Revelation 12:7-12

[10] See Romans 8:31-37; 1 Corinthians 15:57; 2 Corinthians 11:3

There are several ways we may demonstrate our lack of faith in God, live with unhealthy thoughts and behaviors, or fail to agree with Jesus' judgement of our spiritual enemy. The primary ways we do this is through our thoughts, words, actions, and motives.

Lacking Faith in Our Thoughts

Thoughts are the ideas we think, believe, or meditate on or the attitudes we embrace. These thoughts can be about ourselves, others, and God. Paul writes to the Philippian church that we are to think about things that are true, honorable, just, pure, lovely, commendable, excellent, or worthy of praise (Philippians 4:8). Therefore, we empower our spiritual enemy when we do not allow the Holy Spirit to lead our thoughts. Likewise, we do the same with our behavior if it is not life-giving, encouraging, helpful, beneficial, or kind. We agree with destructive lies by declaring ideas over ourselves or others that do not take into consideration who Jesus is or what he has accomplished. Finally, we further separate ourselves from God in believing He is not a good and perfect Heavenly Father or that He does not love and pursue us.

Lacking Faith in Our Words

Our words include anything we audibly say or type, or the tone and style in which we say something. These may be words we say to or about ourselves, others, and God. Paul tells us that our speech is to be gracious, upbuilding, encouraging, consoling, loving, and gentle.[11] We bring death into our relationships when our speech does not line up with God's character and what He says about people; this includes attacks at someone's character or motives. For example, we can destroy someone's reputation or their relationships

---

[11] See Colossians 4:6; 1 Corinthians 14:3; Ephesians 4:15-16; Titus 3:2

through gossip (telling unnecessary or unjustified negative truths about someone) or slander (spreading lies about someone). We can either bring life or death into a relationship with what we say.[12]

Lacking Faith in Our Actions

Our actions include anything we've willfully done, participated in, looked at, or listened to. Our relationship with God and others can struggle when we try to meet our needs and desires outside of or in opposition to how God designed them to be met. We can also negatively affect the relationship other people have with God when we try to "help" them without fully knowing their situation or how God desires to meet their need. Our desire to jump in and fix the problem can actually further complicate their issues. We can hinder their trust in God and compound the problem further when our help is only influenced by what we *think* is good and beneficial rather than the leading and direction of the Holy Spirit. This "help" can stifle His attempt to have a vibrant and interpersonal relationship with that person.

Finally, we can reject relationship with God by not doing something He has asked us to do. By neglecting what the Holy Spirit has put on our mind to do, we are rejecting His grace and empowerment — we are turning down the volume of His voice in our conscience.

Lacking Faith in Our Motives

Our motives are the reason behind what we think, say, and do. Our identity is intrinsic — received from God — and we are created in His image and likeness to reflect Him. Living from this truth will make our thoughts, words, and actions life-giving, healthy, and will be natural to our personal God-given design.

However, if we have a distorted or devalued perception of our identity, our thoughts, words, and actions will be motivated by

---

[12] See James 3:1-12

earning or achieving our identity and worth. Inevitably, our motives will be self-focused, self-reliant, and self-seeking.

HEALTHY & UNHEALTHY GRIEF

In second Corinthians, Paul tells us we have two options when confronted with living and thinking in ways opposed to how we were designed: we can have unhealthy grief or healthy grief (2 Corinthians 7:10-11).

Unhealthy Grief

Unhealthy grief (or worldly sorrow) is *a self-focused regret over one's sins, failures, and mistakes that leads to debilitating shame and anxiety.* It focuses on the personal discomforts and painful consequences of our unhealthy mindsets and behaviors. This unhealthy sorrow perpetuates a stagnant lifestyle (unchanged mindsets and behaviors) that continues to entrap us. This enslavement produces regret, discontentment, and shame. Ultimately, this leads to emotional, relational, mental, and eventually, physical death. Additionally, it breaks relationship and our connection to loved ones and God.[13]

Unhealthy grief may feel bad, regretful, or even apologetic when caught or found out. However, the lifestyle change is either momentary or non-existent. This is because this kind of grief is rooted in a fear of what others think rather than a genuine desire for healthy relationship.[14] It focuses on what people may believe, say, or do to us if our sins, failures, and mistakes were exposed. Additionally, it is a fear of what will happen to us through natural consequences or justifiable punishment. Unhealthy grief seeks justification, manipulation, and self-preservation that results in shame and hopeless regret.

---

[13] See Romans 5:8-11; 12:2; 2 Corinthians 5:18-21; 7:10; Ephesians 2:12
[14] See Proverbs 29:25; Luke 12:4-7

Healthy Grief

Healthy grief (or godly sorrow) is *a genuine, Christ-focused, Spirit-led remorse over one's sins, failures, and mistakes.* It focuses on the relational disconnection or outcomes because of a sin, failure, or mistake. Healthy sorrow leads to a changed lifestyle that promotes health and wholeness. These healthy mindsets produce hope, peace, and joy. Ultimately, this leads to vibrant emotional, relational, mental, and physical health.

Healthy grief thrives in relationship and connection with loved ones and God. It willingly exposes and confesses temptations, struggles, and sins with the goal of living free, restored, and connected. This is because healthy grief is rooted in trusting God over fears of circumstances or other people.[15] It acknowledges our position and status before God and submits to His sovereignty and justice. Healthy grief desires to be in healthy relationship with God above our fear of being punished by Him.

Because God is holy and perfectly loving and merciful, we can be confident in His love for us, His helpful grace, and His desire for our good. We are comforted by God's desire to help us rather than judge us. This kindness is what leads us to repent.[16]

Healthy grief views ourselves in light of God's love, forgiveness, and grace rather than our own thoughts and behaviors. It entrusts our sins, failures, and mistakes — along with their negative effects and consequences — to the Holy Spirit. Through repentance, healthy grief makes a genuine effort toward restitution, reconciliation, and restoration. Our repentance to the Father does not earn us His forgiveness; rather, our repentance is our response to His forgiveness. Healthy grief results with us feeling hopeful, joyful, free, and connected to God and others.[17] Repentance that does not end in hope and joy is either incomplete or a self-focused regret over our thoughts and actions.

---

[15] See Proverbs 1:7; Jeremiah 17:5-8; Luke 12:4-7
[16] See 1 John 4:18; Hebrews 4:16; Acts 9:31
[17] See Galatians 5:11; Luke 15:3-7

———————— // ————————

Repentance resulting from conviction is not simply the avoidance of sin. It is an intentional pursuit of reconciliation with God and others through building new, healthy behaviors in line with our God-given identity. Repentance is a change in our thinking that is proven over time through our behaviors. This Spirit-empowered lifestyle change is what renews, strengthens, and guards our minds.

Second Corinthians 7:11 reveals what healthy grief looks like.[18] It is an *earnest*, diligent, wholehearted authentic concern and effort toward repentance. It is an *eagerness* to clear ourselves of any accusation that we tolerate sinful thoughts and behaviors. It is a deep desire to be reconciled and restored in our relationship with God and others.

Healthy sorrow also exhibits an *indignation* or anger toward sin and its negative effects. It is accompanied by a healthy *fear* of offending God by further rejection of our design and identity through continued sin. This results in a *longing* and hope for healthy relationship and connection; a *zeal* or passion and commitment to make restitution and do what is right.

Finally, healthy sorrow is ready for *punishment* — putting to death any thoughts or behaviors that do not align with and encourage our God-given identity or abilities. This death comes through developing new, healthy mindsets and behaviors.[19] The byproduct of our repentance is our complete innocence before God. This innocence is based in trusting the fact that God has forgiven us.

---

[18] The italicized words are taken from the ESV Bible. Some of this description of 2 Corinthians 7:11 is taken from the Amplified® Bible (AMP), copyright © 2015 by The Lockman Foundation. Used by permission. www.Lockman.org

[19] See 2 Corinthians 10:5-6 to see how we capture and kill every thought not in agreement with our God-given identity and destiny. We kill these lies by meditating on the characteristics listed in Philippians 4:4-8.

ACTIVATION STEP

Pray the following prayer. Be sure to take a few moments after you pray to silently wait for the Holy Spirit to respond. Then, write down what He says or shows you.

"Heavenly Father, thank you for not holding against me the things I have said or done that have hurt You and those around me. Holy Spirit, what sin, failure, or mistake in my life continues to bring up feelings of shame, regret, or guilt?"

"Holy Spirit, I choose to receive Your forgiveness for this behavior. I release to You how my behaviors have negatively affected myself or others. I trust Your mercy and that You can fix and redeem the effects of my unhealthy mindsets and behaviors. Holy Spirit, what do You want me to do when I feel shame, regret, or guilt over this issue?"

Feelings of shame, regret, or guilt can often be a symptom of believing a lie about ourselves or God's character. This lie prevents us from seeing ourselves as God does — hindering our ability to fully receive His forgiveness and love. I encourage you to work through *The Freedom Booklet* in the back of this book. Use what the Holy Spirit revealed to you above as the offense and you being the offender. As you work through the process, He will bring peace and hope to your mind regarding this situation.

CHAPTER SIX

EXPENSE

ACCEPTING THE COST
OF HEALTHY HABITS

Because of the sacrifice of the Messiah,
his blood poured out on the altar of the
Cross, we're a free people — free of
penalties and punishments chalked up
by all our misdeeds. And not just barely
free, either. Abundantly free! He
thought of everything, provided for
everything we could possibly need,
letting us in on the plans he took such
delight in making.

— EPHESIANS 1:7-9, THE MESSAGE

PORNOGRAPHY WAS ONE OF THOSE HABITS THAT OCCUPIED MY MIND NEARLY EVERY WAKING HOUR.

My addiction to pornography began when I was six with an innocent walk in the woods near my house. During this walk I stumbled upon someone's personal stockpile of magazines. While I initially told my parents, the seed had already been implanted in my brain. Through junior high and high school, I had a paper route. On my route was an abandoned garage where I started my own stockpile. I traded various belongings with friends at school for magazines they stole from their dads. This was the foundation to a nearly 20-year addiction.

When Lacey and I were first married, I was in my fourth year of Bible school. I only had morning classes, and with Lacey working until late afternoon most days, I was home alone, free to browse the internet. The addiction had grown into a fantasy that occupied my mind nearly every waking hour. These fantasy hours were also filled with deep shame and regret. The more I looked at and thought about it, the more disgusted with myself I became. I hated myself. To regain some sense of value, I would turn back to pornography — the only thing that gave me a sense of worth and acceptance.

I had always believed that getting married would resolve this dark secret I carried. But it didn't. So, I began to separate my life into two parts — my intimacy with my wife and my thought life with pornography. For me, sex had always been associated with my addiction. While intimacy with my wife should have made me feel loved and accepted, it felt wrong — leaving me feeling gross and disgusted. Yet, my dark secret also left me feeling dirty.

I continued living this divided lifestyle well into our fifth year of marriage. I would look at pornography, "repent," and repeat. By this point, both Lacey and I were on staff at a church. She was the communications director and I was the associate youth pastor. The youth pastor at the time was starting a church in another city and I was in position to take his place. Along with this, Lacey and I were wrestling with infertility as a result of my Cystic Fibrosis. Finally, there were some medical insurance issues that would potentially affect the coverage of some medications that I required to stay alive. It was an incredibly stressful time. I was feeling pressure emotionally, mentally, and physically. To cope, I decided to go to a strip club believing it would relieve some pressure.

It did not.

As I mentioned before, the result of this choice meant that I had to step down as associate youth pastor. Because our house was owned by the church and was part of my compensation, we were also asked to move out. Finally, I was asked to publicly confess to our church — a congregation of nearly 1200 members — because I was a prominent figure on staff. This was, by far, the most humiliating time in my life.

For the first time, my dark secret was known.

Lacey and I went to counseling for nearly a year. Most of this time centered around resolving issues we had from our childhood and learning how to work as a team within our marriage. I realized during this time how to share my feelings and thoughts with Lacey. I learned that my addiction was simply a symptom — a coping behavior for when I felt alone, disconnected, and devalued.

I also began building new habits and behaviors that promoted freedom and intimacy with Lacey. This freedom came at a cost; I had to give up things I felt I had a right to. One example of this is that I no longer had internet on my phone or computer. If someone asked me to look something up on my phone I couldn't. Often, they would press me for a reason since I had a smart phone. I would have to admit I was addicted to pornography and that I didn't have access to the internet anymore.

We also ran a production company at the time. This meant any online audio or video resources I needed would have to wait until

Lacey could be with me. While this time in my life was difficult, humiliating, and painstakingly long, I would not trade it for anything. I learned how to overcome moments of temptation. I learned how to change my environment — getting up and making myself a snack instead of staying at my computer. I would immediately tell Lacey about these temptations and let her know how I felt. I built healthy habits during this season which have stuck with me to this day — habits that went beyond simply doing something different. I began believing something different. This season renewed my mind.

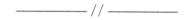

Apart from a miracle, renewing our attitudes, thoughts, beliefs, and behaviors will take time. It is a process, empowered by the Holy Spirit, of building new habits.[1] These new lifestyles aren't simply good works and actions; that would be self-reliant morality.

Morality is *motivation to behave in line with God's design and His kingdom without acknowledging His empowerment.* It either rejects or ignores God's involvement. Morality, void of relying upon God, causes us to strive to be better by doing good and trying harder. This can leave us feeling anxious or judgmental. Spirit-led mindsets and behaviors produce a peace and hope in our minds. Our thoughts will not be plagued with guilt or criticism of others who do not have the same behaviors as us. Spirit-led behaviors are lived out from a place of freedom and rest.

The extent to which we experience real, Spirit-led hope, joy, peace, and freedom depends on how willing we are to allow Him access into our minds. Any area we try to justify, explain, or diminish will be a closed door to the Holy Spirit. Unresolved guilt will lead to regret and shame. This shame leaves us feeling hopeless.

---

[1] Romans 12:1-2; 2 Corinthians 4:16-18; Ephesians 4:17-24; Colossians 3:9-10

However, Nehemiah 8:9-12 explains that our repentance (resolving guilt through a change of mind) and our redemption (building new Spirit-led mindsets and behaviors) lead to joy and celebration rather than regret and shame.

THE COST OF FREEDOM

Our freedom and redemption cost Jesus his life. It will also cost us our comfortable. As we've already discussed, this begins by going back and resolving the events and people that brought about our destructive coping habits. This also means giving up control of what we think should happen or surrendering the attitudes, thoughts, beliefs, or habits that seem natural or normal to us.

Our flesh (specifically our brains and bodies) are what we've habitually inclined toward unnatural and unhealthy desires.[2] When we choose to fulfill our natural, God-given needs and desires in unnatural ways, we develop destructive habits. This creates a draw or connection (i.e., addiction) to unnatural and unhealthy mindsets and behaviors. These unhealthy addictions only lead to increased disappointment.

We transform our destructive desires into life-giving, beneficial ones over time as we build new, Spirit-led mindsets and behaviors. This is how we renew (make new again) our thoughts. Romans 12:1-2 and Colossians 3:9-10 reveal that this transformation will take time and effort. We have to take a proactive approach to our thoughts and actions. Removing these destructive desires may be painful, uncomfortable, or difficult. But it will lead to a freedom and peace that no relationship, possession, or achievement could ever bring.

---

[2] See Romans 1:21-32; Galatians 5:19-21; Ephesians 5:3; Colossians 3:5; James 3:14-15. The Greek word for "flesh", *sarx*, used in these passages is also used in reference to Jesus in John 1:14 and 1 John 4:2. Therefore, it is not our flesh that is inherently sinful. Rather, it is the unnatural and unhealthy desires we have habitually inclined it to that is sinful. See also Matthew 15:18-20.

We are all drawn to different things for different reasons. First John 2:15-17 helps us identify unhealthy and unnatural desires by evaluating how and why we are tempted. The examples I give are only there to help you begin to identify how you might be tempted.

Also, here are a few questions to keep in mind as you read through the types of desires. They will clarify whether your specific desires are healthy or unhealthy.

- *Am I enslaved to my desire for _____ as though I am unable to stop or have no desire to stop my behavior?*

- *Is my desire to _____ and the way I fulfill it encouraging and beneficial for me and those around me?*

- *Are the attitudes, thoughts, and behaviors produced by my desire for _____ healthy for me and those around me?*

Feeling-Based Desires

We were created with feelings and passions. Therefore, these are not innately wrong. However, the desires of the flesh are often the temptations to fulfill our God-given needs and desires apart from His design and provision. It seeks after false peace provided by physical, mental, or social means. In Luke 4:3, we see that Jesus was tempted with this desire when faced with the opportunity to fulfill his hunger pains by turning rocks into bread. Jesus chose to come to earth as a full, flesh and blood human.[3] The plan was for him to live as we all should live — fully submitted to and empowered by the Holy Spirit. Therefore, anything requiring him to access his deity would have been in opposition to God's design and plan. These temptations are often feeling-based and revealed by what brings us pleasure or where we find peace.

A few examples of feeling-based temptations are: 1) emotional fulfillment or sexual arousal from someone other than our spouse; 2) excessive shopping, eating, alcohol, or dieting; 3) immoderate participation in exercise, sporting events, or hobbies; 4) drug or

---

[3] See Philippians 2:5-8; Hebrews 2:14-18

substance abuse; 5) binge watching streaming services, social media, sports, or other forms of escape.

Having-Based Desires

God has given us the created world for our pleasure and fulfillment. However, the desires of the eyes are the temptations to selfishly misuse or overindulge in our Heavenly Father's design and provision. It focuses on temporary pleasures provided by physical, mental, or social means.

We see Jesus, in Luke 4:5-7, tempted with this desire when faced with the opportunity to receive worship without having to suffer or earn it. These temptations are often having-based and revealed by what we are passionate about or preoccupied with.

Examples of having-based temptations include: 1) an unhealthy focus or drive at a career or educational degree; 2) hobbies or activities that steal provision from those we are responsible for taking care of, or that cause disconnection or disunity with those we love; 3) a connection with an animal that sacrifices vulnerable relationship with another human being.

Being-Based Desires

We are created in the image and likeness of God. That is our unchanging identity. Pride is the temptation to achieve worth and value outside of our established God-given identity. While pride can often come off as thinking too highly of ourselves, it is often rooted in being self-deprecating or devaluing one's self. Therefore, the pride of life also applies to those who, while not being outwardly arrogant, still do not believe their worth and value. Often, Christians will use "struggling with pride" as a means of avoiding vulnerability and dealing with the real emotional root issues. While "struggling with pride" may be a real symptom, it insufficiently resolves the underlying issue of a distorted or devalued identity.

These temptations seek to earn approval and worth through physical, mental, or social means. Jesus was tempted with this desire in Luke 4:3 and 9 when faced with the opportunity to prove his identity (his value and worth) through his actions. These temptations are often being-based and revealed by the possessions (or lack of possessions) or positions we seek after (or intentionally turn down) and boast about.

Examples of being-based desires can be similar to the previous two in that there may be similar behaviors but the mindsets behind them are different. We can find value and worth in our jobs, a college degree, our looks, or the people with whom we associate. Additionally, we can even find value and worth in our families, spouse, or children. This desire is perhaps best examined in light of identifying something or someone we cannot live without.

> "[My] freedom came at a cost;
> I had to give up things I felt
> I had a right to."

One final note about this being-based desire is that we can derive a sense of worth and value from not having possessions. Minimalism or a poverty mindset can cause us to develop a false humility, as though we are better because we have less or sacrifice more. This can be as equally pride-filled as those who seek after fame, wealth, and comfort.

The quality of our desire, whether it is healthy or unhealthy, often comes down to our motivation. In the last chapter I told you my story of wanting to be a church planter. For most people, this is a noble calling in which their pursuit often finds them fulfilling the call of God on their life. For me, it was simply trying to make a name for myself — to be someone who was important, valued, and appreciated by people other than my family. I was on a road to emotionally and mentally abandoning my wife and daughters. Had I continued this pursuit, it would have left me empty and alone.

THE PROCESS OF REPENTANCE

In chapter two I defined repentance as the process of building new, Spirit-led mindsets and behaviors over time. It requires us to recognize and realign any attitudes, thoughts, beliefs, or feelings that don't agree with what our Heavenly Father says about us.

Repentance is not the apology or the words and actions toward those we've offended. It is proving over time our changed mindsets through changed behaviors. Additionally, these new habits will solidify the new beliefs we're developing. The process of repentance begins with the Heavenly Father's kindness and grace. This leads to us experiencing His love.

The Process of Repentance – Step #1:
God's Kindness & Patience

God's kindness and patience are the catalyst to our change. He desires us to live free, joy-filled lives empowered by the Holy Spirit.[4] However, our ability to respond to His kindness begins with us recognizing our position before Him.[5]

Our relationship with Him often begins with a healthy fear, respect, and awe of who He is — His majesty, power, and authority. However, a mature relationship with Him is based on being loved by Him rather than fearing Him. Experiencing His love and trusting His goodness is the goal of our relationship with Him. Therefore, feeling loved by Him and loving others is the mark of a mature relationship with Him.[6]

One example of the Father's kindness leading to repentance is the story of Peter found in Luke 5:1-11. Jesus' overwhelming financial blessing (the catch of fish) and kindness brought Peter to a place of conviction and repentance.

---

[4] See Romans 2:4-5; John 12:32.
[5] See Hosea 3:5; Psalm 2:11; Proverbs 1:7
[6] See Matthew 22:34-40; 1 John 2:28-3:24; 4:7-21; Ephesians 3:14-19

The Process of Repentance – Step #2:
The Holy Spirit's Conviction

As we experience and walk in the Father's kindness and love, the Holy Spirit will convict us — revealing areas in our thoughts and behaviors that are in opposition of His love. His conviction goes beyond issues of morality by revealing any mistrust or distrust we have of Him.[7] Additionally, He will convict us of any mindset or behavior that leads to disconnection or disunity with others.

One area this has played out in my marriage is my responsibility for taking out the trash. The trash is not a moral issue. However, when I forget or neglect to do it, my relationship with my wife suffers. Therefore, I have taken intentional steps toward hearing God remind me to take it out in the mornings.

Beyond knowing the Holy Spirit convicts us, we need to understand that we do not *need* to convict others. As we show love, grace, and kindness toward peoples mistakes and failures — rather than judgement and condemnation — we are inviting the Holy Spirit to convict them. There may be times when we do need to directly confront people about their hurtful behavior. However, this should not be our immediate response. Rather than seeking to convince others of their wrongdoing, we need to first seek to make them feel loved and cared for. Then the Holy Spirit *may* lead us to confront.[8] Whatever your personal view of confrontation is, I will discuss the steps to healthy confrontation in chapter ten.

The declaration of sin (or cursing someone[9]) pronounces a judgement and identity over them that only looks at their behavior. While it may describe what someone has done (i.e., someone who steals is often called a thief), it does not take into consideration who they are — the very image and likeness of their Heavenly Father.[10] Additionally, only pointing out the sins, failures, or mistakes of

---

[7] See John 16:7-11
[8] See 1 Corinthians 14:1-4; Ephesians 4:15-16, 25-32
[9] See Romans 3:14; 12:14; James 3:9-10. Cursing is making disparaging, discouraging, or devaluing remarks toward someone or an unfounded accusation of someone.
[10] See James 3:1-12; Galatians 3:10, 13

others does not provide a remedy. It only brings hopelessness and suffering. Cursing someone will result in one of two outcomes: 1) the offended will agree with the accusation made by the offender and continue behaving in line with this distorted identity; 2) the offended will try to prove the offender wrong by doing things in an attempt to achieve an identity higher than the curse. Neither of these are the answers Jesus gave nor do they agree with our God-given identity.

The conviction of the Holy Spirit moves through prophetic words, not declarations of sins. First Corinthians 14:1-5 reveals that a prophetic word is uplifting, encouraging, and consoling. It motivates change through believing the best about someone — seeing them for their God-given identity rather than their destructive activity.

When I was addicted to pornography, the constant shame and guilt I felt was overwhelming. I often felt paralyzed and unable to change because I believed that this addiction was who I was. This was not necessarily improved when I had to confess to the church. Several people after the church service told my wife how disgusting my addiction was and how thankful they were that their husband never struggled with this addiction. It wasn't until my counselor affirmed my God-given identity and the capabilities the Heavenly Father gave me to overcome this addiction that I felt like I could live again. My counselor's encouragement gave me the motivation and desire to change my mindsets and behaviors.

The Process of Repentance – Step #3:
Receive Forgiveness

Misdeeds are *our sins, failures, and mistakes.* While our failures and mistakes are different from our willful sin, they can have the same painful, negative effects, and consequences on people as our sin does. Therefore, we need the same peace, hope, and freedom for our mistakes and failures as we do from our sins. Jesus took our sins, failures, and mistakes upon himself — he became those misdeeds. Dying, Jesus killed them. Raising from the dead, Jesus freed us from them.[11] We are free from the regret, shame, and condemnation those misdeeds have on us. However, we are only free when we resolve the guilt we feel.

Our Heavenly Father, by Jesus, paid for our misdeeds — forgiving them completely, thoroughly, and fully. There is no act of penance or contrition that would make our forgiveness more complete. Furthermore, no amount of forgiving ourselves will bring the resolution and peace we seek. We simply trust and receive the Father's forgiveness. This empowers us to live free from the lies of the enemy about our identity. We will be victorious over the enemy's desire for us to live condemned to false guilt, debilitating regret, paralyzing shame, and hopeless anxiety.[12]

At this point, I feel it necessary to encourage those struggling with guilt, regret, shame, or anxiety to visit *The Freedom booklet* at the back of this book. Work through this resource through the lens of repentance — you as the offending person. Pay special attention to receiving God's forgiveness rather than you forgiving yourself.

The Process of Repentance – Step #4: Our Confession & Vulnerability

Confessing our misdeeds to God goes beyond simply telling Him something He already knows. It is our acknowledgement to Him that we have not been thinking and living in agreement with how He designed us. It is affirming that we have quieted His voice in our mind.[13] Confessing our misdeeds to those we've offended acknowledges that we've hurt them and negatively affected them.[14]

Beyond just confessing our misdeeds to trusted, Spirit-led friends, when we confess our temptations to them as well, we invite their encouragement and accountability.

---

[11] See Romans 8:1; 2 Corinthians 5:21; Galatians 3:13-14
[12] See Matthew 20:28; Romans 4:25; 5:10; 1 Corinthians 15:3; 2 Corinthians 5:11-12; Ephesians 1:7-10; 2:13-22; 4:32; Colossians 1:19-23; Hebrews 9:26; 10:12
[13] See 1 John 1:9
[14] See Matthew 5:23-26

Accountability should not focus on the patterns of failure. Rather, it is an opportunity to give an account of one's ability — focusing on the new mindsets and behaviors we are building.[15]

The Process of Repentance – Step #5:
Our Empowerment & Paying Restitution

Allowing the Holy Spirit to lead us enables us to capture and replace thoughts that are not in agreement with how God designed us or thinks about us.[16] Our willingness to listen for the Spirit's voice in our mind may begin with taking the steps to make amends (pay restitution) to the people we have offended.

Restitution, as far as it is possible, is the responsibility we have to those we've offended. It is not penance (self-inflicted punishment or payment that absolves sin), nor is it a means of earning forgiveness.

Through the years as we've taught our girls how to apologize, there have been times when they've written out their apology with money taped to the note. This written apology usually takes the form of the question, "Will you forgive me?" with check "yes" or "no" boxes. We always reject this payoff and reteach them forgiveness is unearned. As they've realized that their money won't buy our forgiveness, the monetary incentives have stopped. Restitution should not be used to receive forgiveness. However, it is our responsibility as the offender to do our best to make amends through offering reasonable restitution.[17]

A friend of mine, when he was younger, was with some friends and they threw rocks at an old church's stained-glass windows. The windows shattered and the kids ran off. Later, when my friend was in ministry school, the Holy Spirit convicted him of this offense. He knew that complete freedom from this event would only

---

[15] See Mark 1:5; Acts 19:18; James 5:16. Jesus encouraged Peter in Luke 22:31-34 to get back into relationship with the other disciples to confess, encourage, and strengthen them.
[16] See Galatians 5:16-26; Luke 22:31-32 (especially 22:32b); Philippians 4:8
[17] See Exodus 22:1-15; Numbers 5:5-7; Matthew 5:21-26; 2 Corinthians 7:10-11

happen if he pursued making restitution for the church. However, he knew that replacing the stained-glass would have cost thousands of dollars. He nervously contacted the current pastor and told him the story and apologized for what he had done. Reluctantly he then offered to pay for the windows he had broken. In a complete act of mercy on the part of the pastor, he declined my friend's offer. While my friend didn't end up needing to make restitution, he knew he had to offer it to receive peace from the pain of this memory.

While we may fully receive the Father's forgiveness and make adequate restitution, we may still have consequences to live with because of our mindsets and behaviors. These consequences, in no way, should be taken as punishment from God or a representation of how He feels toward us. They are simply the natural result of a bad choice; it is the restitution that must be paid to society, culture, or an organization for our misdeeds negatively affects.

When I confessed to going to a strip club as a youth pastor, the consequences required me to be released from a leadership position in the church. Living that out was painful, uncomfortable, and out of my control. It also affected other people in my life including my friends and especially my wife. But, God honored my submission to the leadership of this church and their process. He continues to use the memory of these consequences as a motivator in my freedom and wholeness. Furthermore, this church continues to be one of the most generous financial supporters of our ministry.

ACTIVATION STEP

Pray the following prayer. Be sure to take a few moments after you pray to silently wait for the Holy Spirit to respond. Then, write down what He says or shows you.

"Heavenly Father, thank You for choosing to have mercy on me. Jesus, I desire to be in right relationship with you and those I've hurt or offended. Holy Spirit, who is one person I need to apologize to and make things right with?"

"Holy Spirit, I know that I'm not responsible for how the other person will respond to my apology. But, as far as it depends on me, beyond apologizing for my behavior, what can I do or say to show this person I am willing to make restitution?"

In the next few days, seek this person out and apologize. Ask them how you might be able to make amends — as far as you are able and is reasonable. Offer as restitution what the Holy Spirit revealed to you above. Be sure to seek His wisdom and guidance through this process.

Next, if you know that your hurtful behavior is habitual, seek out a life-giving, Spirit-filled friend who will encourage you and strengthen you through the process of building new mindsets and behaviors. Ask them to hold you accountable for the positive changes you are making.

CHAPTER SEVEN

AWARE

TURNING BAD HABITS
INTO GOOD ONES

No test or temptation that comes your
way is beyond the course of what
others have had to face. All you need
to remember is that God will never let
you down; he'll never let you be pushed
past your limit; he'll always be there to
help you come through it.

— 1 CORINTHIANS 10:13, THE MESSAGE

NOT ONLY DID IT BREAK MY PRIDE, IT BROKE MY TWO FRONT TEETH.

I liked soccer. But more than that, I liked girls. And for a pre-teen boy, what better distraction was there than girls playing soccer.

I was about 10 years old when I noticed a soccer match happening across the street from my house. We lived next to the elementary school where there were often baseball, football, and soccer games happening. We had just finished dinner when I noticed the soccer match. I also noticed that it was a girl's league.

My interest was piqued.

I told my mom that I just wanted to ride my bike around the block before bedtime — strategically leaving out the fact that there were dozens of girls across the street who I needed to check out.

I hopped on my bike and began to ride. I made sure to stay on the closest side of the street, nearest the field, while also trying to stay out of the way of traffic. I didn't want to get hit while I gazed upon all the girls.

I slowly made my way down the street, passing the first field where several teams were practicing. I was moving way too fast to get a good look, so I slowed down. As I neared the second field, I looked back for one more glance. *So many pretty girls*— BAM!

My face met the back end of a parked truck so hard that one of my teeth was nearly knocked out and the other one chipped in half.

The man had obviously been sitting in his truck because he came out yelling. "What do you think you're doing hitting my truck —," He paused mid-holler, seeing me holding my bloody face. I held my hands in front of my face acting like I was trying to catch the blood all the while just hiding my shame and embarrassment.

It wasn't too long before a nice crowd began to form around me — mostly made up of the girls I was, moments earlier, gazing at. I was completely mortified. They asked if I was okay, to which I responded that I was. I had to play it cool despite all the tears, blood, and drool running down my face. I picked up my bike and began walking home. Still not wanting anyone to know who I was or where I lived, I rode my bike — bloody, throbbing face, and all — around the entire block of the school.

I had seen the parked cars when I began my ride and would have sworn to anyone who asked that I was at least a half a block away from them. But, I was completely unaware of how quickly I was moving toward the parked truck because I was sidetracked by the girls playing soccer. Had I been more aware of my surroundings I would have noticed the danger I was heading toward. We can get so sidetracked by our circumstances — and feelings of disappointment and frustration — that we lose track of how our own unhealthy mindsets and behaviors can hurt us.

Once we've truly received the Heavenly Father's forgiveness, we can begin to build new habits and behaviors based upon grace and freedom rather than guilt and shame. These new healthy behaviors can help promote new healthy mindsets.

Paul tells us in first Corinthians 10:12 that we are to be aware of our common weaknesses so that we don't fall. We can identify these specific weaknesses by recognizing our common temptations and acknowledging the ways we usually give into those temptations. Once we've discovered these common weaknesses, we can pre-determine our next response — choosing to live in agreement with our God-given identity and ability.

What we think and believe about ourselves — our identity and abilities — will determine how successful we are at developing new life-giving behaviors. Who we believe we are will determine what we think we can do or not do. Therefore, how we perceive our identity will influence our activity. If we believe we are merely

wretched depraved sinners saved by grace, we will approach
temptation as a defeated sinner. Our true identity is that of a
victorious conqueror with Jesus. We are empowered by the same
Spirit who raised Jesus from the dead. He lives in us.[1]

HOW WE DEVELOP UNHEALTHY HABITS

We were created with natural, God-given desires, needs, and
appetites. Unhealthy desires usually begin to develop in our early
childhood years. They usually begin as coping mechanisms for
when our family members, peers, and authority figures neglect,
reject, or overtly abuse or misuse their God given role and
responsibility. Their negative examples influence the unhealthy
desires we begin to crave. These desires become "natural" to us as
we give into them. They become normal thought patterns and
lifestyles. The following is the progression of how unhealthy
desires take root in our mind and develop into our behaviors.

Developing Unhealthy Habits - Step #1:
Our God-Given Needs & Desires

Desires are strong passionate feelings of wanting or needing
someone or something or wanting something to happen. **Desire** is
*neither good or bad — it is simply a craving or longing to fulfill a perceived need
we have.*[2] The object of or method in which we fulfill these desires
is what matters. Often our desires start out as signals of an
unfulfilled God-given need (e.g., hunger, thirst, love, connection,
affirmation, etc.). For example, if we do not feel loved or affirmed
in our early growing up years, we will seek love and affirmation
through unhealthy means. We will connect with unhealthy people

---

[1] See Romans 8:11,37; Galatians 1:1; 1 Corinthians 15:57; 1 John 5:4
[2] The Greek words translated "earnestly desire" that Jesus feels in Luke 22:15 is *epithymia
epithymeo*. *Epithymia* is the same word translated in James 1:15 as "desire". This reveals that
simply having desire does not mean it is unhealthy. Rather, it is the object of our desire than
may be unhealthy.

who affirm our unnatural and destructive lifestyles; we will fight and argue to gain respect and affirmation; or we will withdraw, isolating ourselves and becoming depressed. In either case, we increase our feelings of loneliness and being uncared for or unloved.

In the last chapter I listed a few questions to keep in mind regarding desires. I recommend revisiting those questions when you are confused or uncertain about whether a desire you have is healthy or unhealthy.

Developing Unhealthy Habits - Step #2: Temptation to Fulfill Our Needs in Unhealthy Ways

Temptations begin as an external influence (by another person or spirit, as a thought in our mind).[3] **Temptation** is *an attempt to persuade, induce, entice, or rouse desire through invitation or attraction.* Similar to desire, temptation is not a bad thing. It is the object of our temptation that can be unhealthy. Therefore, unhealthy temptations are an invitation to live either independent or co-dependent upon God and others; fulfilling our God-given needs and desires outside of His design and provision.

For example: 1) the need for food turns into gluttony, bulimia, or anorexia; 2) the idea of alcohol leads to drunkenness or a legalistic abhorrence of it; 3) the need for love and connection becomes the desire for pornography, multiple sexual partners, homosexuality, gender confusion, and other unhealthy, unnatural sexual expressions, etc. Additionally, the need for relationship can lead us to manipulating and controlling those around us (including God) to get what we want. We either isolate from people or demand that people give us what we feel is lacking. Our desire for others to provide for our God-given needs (feeling loved, connected, and cared for) is not a right we can demand.

Using the metaphor of trees to represent our lives, our destructive behaviors (i.e., giving into unhealthy temptations) is the

---

[3] See Genesis 4:6-7; Matthew 18:6; Mark 9:42; Luke 17:2; Galatians 6:12

fruit of our lives. This fruit draws nutrients from the root systems of our minds (i.e., our negative thoughts and feelings) and promotes our unhealthy lifestyles. This root system of thinking begins with as a seed — an experience or relationship in our early childhood that made us believe we were unloved, uncared for, or unsafe.

Ultimately, unhealthy temptations are the opportunity to reject God's design and provision as the ultimate source of joy, worth, acceptance, love, and safety.

Developing Unhealthy Habits - Step #3: Developing Unhealthy Behaviors

As I mentioned before, the Bible often uses the terms sin, unrighteousness, and ungodliness interchangeably.[4]   However, based upon John 16:8-10, Romans 1:18; and 14:23, we can define sin as the broad description of our intentional or unintentional distrust or mistrust of God expressed in our misdeed and unhealthy behaviors.[5] Therefore, sin is deeper than simply our words and actions. It is rooted in our mind from the examples of unhealthy relationships and interactions modeled to us.

Giving ourselves over to unhealthy and unnatural mindsets and behaviors is the pivotal point in developing habitual inclinations. If we look at temptation as the "first thought" we have — something out of our control — our decision to behave in an unhealthy way is our "second thought." This decision to give into the first thought reinforces the unhealthy mindsets we've developed. Our brains become enslaved (bonded or addicted) to these destructive attitudes, thoughts, and behaviors. When we embrace these "second thoughts" we form unhealthy habits. This is what the Bible refers to as becoming depraved — corrupt in our mindsets and behaviors.[6]

---

[4] See John 16:8-10; Romans 1:18, 14:23; 1 Timothy 1:9; 1 Peter 4:18; Jude 14-18
[5] See John 8:34; Romans 3:23; 6:16-20; 2 Peter 2:19
[6] See 2 Chronicles 36:13; Job 9:4; Psalm 95:8; Proverbs 28:14; Ezekiel 18:24, 26; Isaiah 53:6; John 8:34; Romans 1:20-23; 6:16-19; Ephesians 4:17-19; Hebrews 3:8-15; 2 Peter 2:19 — pay special attention to the words "became", "become", "hardened", and "turns".

Developing Unhealthy Habits - Step #4:
Death of Our Emotions, Mind, & Relationships

Physical death is the consequence of the original humans rebelling against their God-given design and destiny. As a result, creation has passed on a bent toward death and decay — a "death DNA" if you will. This "death DNA" causes us to develop and pass on diseases, succumb to gestational issues or chemical imbalances, and ultimately die.[7] Our choice to give into unhealthy temptations can expedite this physical death in both ourselves and others (e.g., disease, drug overdose, alcohol poisoning, murder, etc.). In addition to this physical death — and equally devastating — we can cause emotional, mental, and relational death within ourselves and others.

Emotional death is *developing unhealthy and destructive attitudes that are not in line with God's design for us.* This may include "numbing out" or having little to no emotional response to life. Conversely, we may also overreact emotionally to an event or person. This type of emotional death can cause us to manipulate people into giving us the response we desire — using our emotions as a weapon to get what we want rather than seeing them as a signal to address an unmet need. In either case, it is a death of how God designed our emotions to work and thrive.

---

[7] See Romans 5:12; 1 Corinthians 15:22. God created Adam and Eve, with a world full of good, healthy, life-giving choices. God allowed an alternative option to provide the opportunity to test their love and strengthen their trust in God. It was a choice designed to increase their endurance, character, hope, and their faith in their Heavenly Father. This testing of their faith would have eventually produced a steadfastness that resulted in the perfect completeness of God's design for them (James 1:2-4). Unfortunately, when faced with the opportunity to trust their God-given identity and ability, they chose to doubt. It was this act of distrusting God that led to the consequence of physical death (Genesis 3:18-19, 22-24; see also Ezekiel 18:1-32; Romans 5:12-14, 17; 8:19-23; 1 Corinthians 15:1-22, 50) and the "Death DNA". In removing the Tree of Life, God graciously allows us to die physically, removing the possibility of us living forever separated from Him because of our cursed and imperfect physical bodies. It is only through repentance and submission to the Holy Spirit that we are empowered to be resurrected from this death to live forever with Him (1 Corinthians 15:50; John 3:3, 5).

Mental death is *developing thoughts and beliefs about ourselves, others, and God that are not in line with God's character, design, or plan.* This may include believing we are not worthy of God's sacrifice, assuming the worst about people's actions and motives, or believing God is not perfect, loving, and good. Mental death destroys our ability to have encouraging, life-giving thoughts and assumptions about life.

> "Our wholeness... is both a spiritual work and practical work."

Relational death is *withdrawing, ignoring, or overwhelming a relationship to the point of disinterest or disconnection.* It is living co-dependent (believing our identity, worth, and abilities are inseparable from other people) or independent (believing we do not need nor are we influenced by the words and actions of other people). Whatever relational death may look like in our lives, the result is always the same: separation, divorce, unresolved or unrealized conflict, offense, and an unwillingness to forgive.

HOW WE BREAK UNHEALTHY HABITS

Victory over temptation and the enemy[8] comes through building new, healthy mindsets. We build these mindsets by actively listening to the Holy Spirit's voice — a cognitive moment-by-moment decision to trust Him instead of our negative mindsets and emotions. Thankfully, over time this decision to listen to the Holy Spirit leads to healthy thoughts and feelings.

Being emotionally and mentally free of past sins, failures, and mistakes takes receiving the Father's forgiveness. This freedom will promote healthy mindsets and behaviors. Living free is not a

---

[8] See Matthew 13:39; Galatians 6:12

decision made amidst feelings or in light of past choices — it is a cognitive decision, a choice to listen and believe what God says about us in the moment. It trusts the Holy Spirit's prompting despite how we may feel. The following are steps we must take in gaining freedom in our mind and life.[9]

Breaking Unhealthy Habits - Step #1: Acknowledge the Temptation[10]

Acknowledging and vocalizing the temptation in the moment (and later to a trusted, Spirit-led friend or spouse) will help validate, in our mind, the fact that we are being tempted. It will no longer be a thought that haphazardly popped into our brain. In legitimizing this thought through our words, we are acknowledging this idea for what it is — a lie. This affirmation of the lie will encourage us to respond accordingly.[11]

Breaking Unhealthy Habits - Step #2: Identify Our Bait[12]

Being able to identify when, where, and how we are usually tempted will encourage us to be on guard. Assessing our sleep patterns, eating habits, emotional status, and stress levels during a temptation will help us develop a proactive plan with practical steps. We will be aware and able to avoid or appropriately respond to the people or circumstances that are the source of the temptation.

---

[9] See Nehemiah 4:1-14; Romans 6:1-14; 1 Corinthians 6:19-20; Galatians 2:20; 5:1, 16-25; Ephesians 3:14-21; Philippians 4:8; Colossians 2:15; James 1:12-15; 4:71; Peter 5:8; 12:2; Revelation 12:10-11
[10] See 2 Corinthians 10:5-6
[11] See 2 Corinthians 10:5-6 to see how we capture and kill every thought not in agreement with our God-given identity and destiny. We kill these lies by meditating on the characteristics listed in Philippians 4:4-8.
[12] See 1 Corinthians 10:13

Breaking Unhealthy Habits - Step #3:
Recognize Habitual Responses[13]

As we've grown up we've physically wired our brains — through chemically bonded neural connections — to react to specific ideas, people, or circumstances in a particular way. These reactions may have even developed into physical muscle memories (e.g., eye twitches, reactionary flinches, punching, or other gestures, etc.). This entire process is called addiction.

Colossians 3:9 uses the words "old self" and "practices" to describe this process of addiction. The **old self** is simply *the specific lies or common threads of wrong belief we have about ourselves, others, and God* — our unhealthy mindsets. Our **practices** are *our specific unnatural and destructive habitual actions* — our unhealthy behaviors. Therefore, our behaviors become our addiction — the people, places, or things we use to cope with or medicate our negative feelings. Recognizing these familiar practices will enable us to intentionally look for and hear from the Holy Spirit for new, life-giving truth and responses. This includes evaluating earlier attempts to overcome temptations and why they failed.

Breaking Unhealthy Habits - Step #4:
Determine & Prepare Next Response[14]

Temptations often feel like a surprise. However, knowing how we are usually tempted can help us create a predetermined response for the future. This is where developing healthy "second thoughts" takes place; that is, thoughts or beliefs we intentionally bring to mind to combat the "first thought" temptations. These "second thought" responses include vulnerability with others and genuinely seeking the Holy Spirit to speak truth into where and why we are being tempted. This response may include calling someone or changing our circumstances or environment.

---

[13] See Colossians 3:9
[14] See Galatians 5:16; Ephesians 4:24

When I was pursuing freedom from my pornography addiction, I would often get up and go for a walk when tempted. Changing what I was doing would derail the thought and allow me time and space to figure out why I was being tempted.

If you can prepare and pre-determine your next response — plan how you will change your environment — your chances of being free from that temptation will dramatically increase.

Breaking Unhealthy Habits - Step #5:
Find an Encouragement Partner[15]

Being tempted is NOT wrong, sinful, or bad. However, these temptations can often leave us feeling condemned or back at square one. When we tell a trusted, Spirit-led friend or spouse about our temptation, we invite their support and help; they can encourage us to overcome the temptation and live victoriously. This encouragement comes through developing a practical plan — within reason and within our ability — to be victorious amid temptation. This person will become our *Encouragement Partner*.

As Christians, we are often told to seek out an accountability partner — someone to hold us accountable. While the original intent of this relationship may have been positive, too often it fails because it focuses on the negative. Over time, this negative focus and the ensuing negative feelings will inhibit our desire to meet. Accountability focused on negativity only results in disillusionment and failure. This is why we have reimagined a different kind of relationship.

An *Encouragement Partner* will intentionally affirm your God-given identity, focus on preemptive planning within your capabilities, and celebrate victories as you achieve your goals. It is a person we willingly give access and permission to speak into a specific situation in our lives either to help us overcome a struggle or achieve a personal goal. This may be more than one person

---

[15] See 1 Thessalonians 2:13; 5:14; Hebrews 10:25

depending on the area of our life we need help. For example, we could have one *Encouragement Partner* for finances, another for relationships, and one for health. Regardless of what the reason is for having this person in your life, conversations with this person should focus on our victories, the reasons we are victorious, and what we plan to do to cultivate these victories.

As we are vulnerable with our *Encouragement Partner* they have permission to be honest with us about our mindsets, choices, and behaviors. This means giving them full access to be able to speak into our lives as well as seek advice, inviting other Spirit-led people into the situation, and making choices on our behalf that create the opportunity for change in our lives.

Breaking Unhealthy Habits - Step #6:
Renewing Our Mind[16]

Regardless of whether we feel it, we must affirm and agree with God for our identity — we are created in His image and likeness. This is the definition of **humility**, *agreeing with God for who we are and what we can do*, regardless of what we think about ourselves or what others have said about us.

We are more than conquerors who have overcome our sins, failures, and mistakes. We are dead to these unhealthy mindsets and behaviors. The fullness of God lives within us. We have the same mind, thoughts, and beliefs Jesus did when he lived on earth. We agree with God by verbally affirming our identity.

One way we renew our mind is by telling others about the freedom the Holy Spirit has given us. Telling others about our misdeeds is not dwelling on the past. It is an intentional conversation focused on our freedom — being appropriately vulnerable and sharing details that will comfort and encourage those still struggling to be free.

---

[16] See Psalm 1:1-2; 77:12; 119:15; Romans 6:11; 8:11, 37; 12:2; 1 Corinthians 2:16; Ephesians 2:10; 4:23-24; Philippians 4:8; Revelation 12:11

Sharing our story of freedom should provide others with practical avenues to their own freedom. Often we can avoid sharing embarrassing or vulnerable details because there is still shame attached. Many Christians have the idea that their past is "under the blood." Therefore, they avoid sharing details about their story because they believe focusing on the past hinders their ability to move forward. But the fact is, focusing on our past — resolving the pain, shame, and guilt attached to certain events and people — is what leads us to freedom. Sharing the messy details of our story of freedom only promotes more freedom in the future. This freedom isn't just for us; we bring freedom to people's lives when we share our freedom story.

Renewing our mind is a process that takes place through suffering. While God may not be the source of our tests, trials, and temptations, He will certainly use them to strengthen our faith.

Tests are used to reveal the capacity of our faith in the Heavenly Father. They reveal what we believe about God and His character. Failing a test reveals a lack of understanding of His character. Passing a test requires us to expand our knowledge of Him through reading the Bible and listening to the Holy Spirit.[17]

Trials are often used to reveal the quality of our faith. They reveal the motivation of our mindsets — the extent to which our behaviors reflect our faith in God's goodness and provision. Failure in a trial reveals a lack of genuine love and trust in the Father. To pass a trial, all our actions and intentions must be from a mindset that acknowledges, seeks after, and is thankful to Him.[18]

Temptations reveal our commitment to our faith in the Heavenly Father. They also reveal areas in our beliefs and behaviors that we have not allowed the Holy Spirit access. Failure with a temptation reveals a lack of trust in God's provision, character, and design. To pass a temptation, our "second thought" (our response to the initial temptation) must reveal our reliance

---

[17] See Romans 12:2; 2 Corinthians 13:5; Hebrews 3:8; 11:17; James 1:3-8
[18] See 1 Corinthians 3:12-15; James 1:12-15; 1 Peter 1:6-7; 4:12-13

upon and agreement with God's provision, character, and design.

Without tests, trials, and temptations, our faith would atrophy — become weak and useless. I recently had emergency surgery. After spending several days in bed, waiting for the anesthesia to wear off, I tried to stand up. My legs were tired and weak. It took several weeks for me to feel comfortable and get back to a feeling of normalcy when I walked. Our faith is like our leg muscles. It needs something to push against, something to cause our faith to work. This is how our faith gets strengthened.

We can enhance this faith-building process by putting life-giving, Spirit-led content into our minds — submitting all of our thoughts to Jesus. Paul writes to the Philippian church that we do this by meditating on things that are true, honorable, just, pure, lovely, commendable, excellent, and praiseworthy (Philippians 4:8).

Breaking Unhealthy Habits - Step #7:
Resist the Enemy[19]

When we intentionally listen for the Holy Spirit, He provides options of escape and empowers us to withstand any attack on our mind. Therefore, we must be willing to allow the Holy Spirit full access to our mind and behaviors. Our willingness for Him to reveal — often through those close to us — our blind spots, misdeeds, and unforgiven offenses will lead us to thorough freedom and victory.

It is helpful to keep in mind that the enemy is a created finite being, incapable of being all-knowing and all-present. He will not always be attacking. Also, he will allow us to self-destruct — carrying out the behaviors that destroy our mind and relationships.

Our ability to recognize that we are not tempted by everything helps us save our energy for the things that truly tempt us. For example, as a person with a chronic lung disease, I am not tempted by smoking or inhaled substances. They have no appeal to me.

---

[19] See James 4:7; 1 Peter 5:9

Therefore, the enemy will not tempt me in this area. But, I am also well aware of the areas I do know he will tempt me — areas I have been weakened to and taken over by in the past.

We are free. We are victorious. By trusting the Holy Spirit, we no longer need to be overcome by unhealthy mindsets and behaviors. Our wholeness (this freedom and victory) is both a spiritual work and practical work. It is spiritual in that we need to entrust our past sin to Jesus, receiving the Father's forgiveness, and live empowered by the Holy Spirit. We need to believe our God-given identity. I address the practical aspect of our wholeness throughout later chapters.

It is our responsibility to fill our mind with godly, life-giving Scripture, relationships, and influences. The Spirit will give us practical weapons that we must use to fight against negative thoughts, lies, and false beliefs. As we walk in agreement with the Holy Spirit, we will not sin. Furthermore, we will not need to sin.

We have been filled and empowered by God Himself to overcome sin. Therefore, as we make practical changes in our mindsets and behaviors, we will find that our thoughts and beliefs change. They will become encouraging, life-giving, and hopeful.

ACTIVATION STEP

Pray the following prayer. Be sure to take a few moments after you pray to silently wait for the Holy Spirit to respond. Then, write down what He says or shows you.

"Heavenly Father, thank You for helping me overcome my weaknesses, failures, and mistakes. What unhealthy mindset or behavior do I need help getting rid of?"

"Holy Spirit, who is someone I can invite into this area of my life as an Encouragement Partner to help me change this weakness, failure, or mistake?"

In the next few days, ask this person if they would like to help you by becoming your *Encouragement Partner* for the changes you would like to make. It may be beneficial for them to read *Step Five: Find An Encouragement Partner*, so that you both enter this relationship with the same expectations. Plan to meet with this person at least once a week over the next four weeks. When you meet, be sure to develop a detailed plan of action for you to follow. Check in with them every few days for the first couple weeks to share the changes you are making and how you are dealing with those changes.

CHAPTER EIGHT

ASSUME

BELIEVING THE BEST
DESPITE THE WORST

If a hostile witness stands to accuse someone of a wrong, then both parties involved in the quarrel must stand in the Presence of GOD before the priests and judges who are in office at that time. The judges must conduct a careful investigation; if the witness turns out to be a false witness and has lied … give him the same medicine he intended for the other party.

— DEUTERONOMY 19:16-21, THE MESSAGE

I ASKED OUR BABYSITTER IF WE WERE GOING TO GET TOGETHER LATER.

After the whole debacle of confessing my sexual addiction, being let go as the associate youth pastor, and walking through a year of counseling, the church hired me on as the media and communications director. It was a behind the scenes position that helped us pay our housing expenses. Also, I could continue to build healthy habits and mindsets while continuing to serve the church.

One of the big undertakings I started was redesigning the church's stage. This meant getting rid of a huge 50-foot by 30-foot peach-colored curtain that hung on the back of the stage wall. It was hideous. It also meant painting the entire back wall and side walls — nearly 3000 square feet — black. However, there was a catch. We had ministries that met in the main auditorium Monday night through Sunday morning. This mean it all had to be done, painted, and dry by Monday night.

Thankfully, I had arranged for a painter in the church to help me. He and I picked up all the supplies and planned to meet back at the church around midnight to get the project done. At the same time, I had arranged for me and Lacey to go on a date that Sunday evening. I planned it all out and scheduled the babysitter.

While Lacey and I were on our date, I left my phone on just in case our babysitter needed to get a hold of us. I was also texting the painter with final details about the stage project we were doing that evening. The last text I wrote before Lacey and I settled into our date was, "I look forward to getting together with you later."

Send.

About 10 minutes later our babysitter texted me.

"I'm assuming, as you are out on a date with your wife, that your last text wasn't for me."

I was mortified. I immediately texted back affirming her assumption and told her what had happened.

Lacey thought the whole exchange was hilarious.

The fact is, our babysitter knew my story. She knew my struggles. She knew about my addiction. It was a text that, had she overreacted and contacted the pastors rather than me, could have destroyed my marriage and job. But it didn't because she assumed the best about me. She tested her assumption by asking me who the text was meant for. Her response de-escalated the conversation rather than complicating it further.

Our assumptions about people are like a courtroom. Exodus 20:16 tells us not to bear false witness against our neighbor.[1] Bearing false witness is giving an inaccurate, invalid, or incomplete testimony about someone. It is the unfounded and untested story we tell ourselves (or others) about someone's thoughts and behaviors. We can use their behavior as evidence to prove our negative assumptions. Then, based on the evidence, we become the arguing attorney, star witness, judge, and jury for what we believe happened. These assumptions become the judgements we make about a person's character and identity. They become the motivating factor in our interactions (or lack thereof) with the person. We dole out what we believe to be a just and fair response to a person's words and actions. However, testing our assumptions — having a conversation with the person — gives them the opportunity to explain or defend their behavior.

When we assume the best, we believe that a person's actions are either not what they appear to be or perhaps it is something painful in the person's mind that is causing them to respond with such negative behavior. Judging a person solely by their actions is

---

[1] See also Deuteronomy 19:16-20; Proverbs 19:5, 9; 21:28; 24:28; 25:18; Zechariah 8:16; Ephesians 4:25

only half the story. Often, we may not even understand our own actions. Or, we behave in a certain way because of a deep-rooted insecurity or unmet need such as feeling cared for and loved.

Jesus affirms that our attitudes, thoughts, and beliefs about a person will influence how we interact with them. In Matthew 12:33-37 and 15:18 he tells us that our actions proceed from our heart (the deepest part of our belief system).

If we assume the worst about someone — believing who they are is based upon their behaviors — then we will believe the worst about their intentions and motives. Even their healthy, God-given abilities and talents will be viewed through this skewed lens — believing they are selfish, self-gratifying, or self-promoting. We will condemn their good and healthy behavior as prideful or self-seeking. However, if we believe a person's identity is made in the image and likeness of God, then we will assume the best about them. Their actions will only be a symptom of brokenness in their own mind and life.

While a person's actions and words do reveal something about their motivations, often a person's deepest intentions are beyond even their own understanding. This is why Scripture tells us that God alone is the best judge of a person's mind.[2] Our role is to assume the best about them — agreeing with God for their identity and who they truly are. This leads to a grace-filled, Spirit-led, and life-giving response to their behaviors.

Any thought we have about a person that does not agree with God's design of them or the ability of the Holy Spirit to empower them is a false assumption. These false assumptions only steal, kill, and destroy the person's ability to see their God-given identity and live in agreement with it.

---

[2] See Jeremiah 17:5-10. The Lexham English Septuagint translates Jeremiah 17:9 as, "The heart is deeper than all things; a person is also. And who will understand him?" The Septuagint of the Old Testament: English Translation renders Jeremiah 17:9 as, "The heart is deep beyond all things, and it is the man, and who can know him?" These reveal our heart to be more like a deep mysterious abyss rather than deceitfully sick. The last part of the verse reveals the accuracy of these renderings in asking, *who can know or understand it?* The answer comes in verse 10, only God can fully know and understand.

ASSUME THE BEST

Our thoughts, beliefs, and assumptions toward others should always build them up, be encouraging, and filled with grace.[3] Choosing to believe the best — having gracious assumptions — about others does not deny reality. It does, however, choose to trust the Holy Spirit's ability to empower them. We can have this mindset because we know the Heavenly Father desires and pursues relationship with every person. We believe in the Holy Spirit's ability to convict and their ability to respond.

Our assumptions — whether encouraging or discouraging — will affect how we live in relationship with others. Assuming the best builds people up, encouraging them toward their God-given identity and abilities. With this in mind, there are three rules we must be aware of and live by when it comes to our assumptions.

Assumptions – Rule #1: Be Aware of Them

Our brains are wired to make assumptions about the people and the world around us. We develop and rightly prove most of these assumptions in our early developmental years through the circumstances we experience and people we observe — most notably, our parents, family members, and peers. We use this knowledge to develop assumptions about people's intentions and motives without thinking about it.

Our brain is constantly making and working from unconscious assumptions. When we lived in Ireland, I was often confused as to how the roads were designed. They were unnecessarily curvy and often felt like they meandered. I finally asked a friend why the roads seemed so chaotic and precarious. He told me that many of the roads were built up over the centuries from old sheep paths. What started out as narrow herding paths eventually turned into wagon trails and finally narrow two-lane roads. This is how our

---

[3] See Ephesians 4:29-32 and 1 Corinthians 14:1-3

unconscious assumptions develop in our brains — repeated moments of neural connections over time that turn into super-highways of thought patterns and mindsets. Every time we sit down in a chair without first inspecting it, we are working from an assumption that the chair will hold us — a road system of neural connections built up from our experiences. This assumption has been proven by the thousands of chairs that we have sat in over the course of our life.

Unconscious assumptions enable our brains to conserve energy by focusing on the most important tasks — preventing our brains from becoming paralyzed by the millions of calculations and decisions it needs to make on a regular basis. Our brains will always choose the path of least resistance when it comes to decision-making; an unconscious assumption is that path.

Assumptions – Rule #2: Be Gracious with Them

We all make assumptions about people — developing unconscious rules for how we believe they should behave. We assume they will act in a way that agrees with the family and culture in which we grew up. For example, in America you either shake hands or hug when you meet someone. If you're from Alaska, you take your shoes off when you enter a house or you leave them on if you're from Texas.

Most of our assumptions have little effect on our relationships until someone breaks one of these unconscious rules. When this happens, we make negative assumptions about their motives and behaviors — assuming the worst about people based upon our own unresolved negative experiences. We do this to protect ourselves from being hurt. Our brains use these assumptions as a signal to fight or flee from what is causing this pain. While this is a normal and natural response to being hurt, it can also be unconsciously destructive in the context of relationships.

Our assumptions can either bring hope and life to people around us or they bring condemnation and death. Therefore, it is important to keep in mind whether our assumptions are encouraging or discouraging. Gracious assumptions believe the best about someone's motives and behaviors.

> "If we believe a person's identity is made in the image and likeness of God, then we will assume the best about them."

Assumptions – Rule #3: Be Willing to Test Them

Our willingness to talk to the person about our assumptions will give them the opportunity to clarify their actions or intentions. This is not meant to be a confrontational encounter. Rather, it is a conversation that serves only to bring clarity and understanding to you and them. Then, as the Holy Spirit prompts us, we are to bring comfort or correction to their mindsets and behaviors.

Asking genuine questions is a great way to test our assumptions. For example, if we wave at someone and they don't wave back, rather than believe they are mad at us we can test our assumption by simply asking them if they are okay. They may be thinking about something else or focused on a goal and simply didn't see us. This is a positive way to test a potentially negative assumption about someone. Our untested assumptions about a person's motives, abilities, and desires will lead to unhealthy expectations of them. Therefore, having a conversation with them is how we test our assumptions and clarify our expectations.

DEVELOPING HEALTHY EXPECTATIONS

Once we've tested our assumptions, we can build healthy, grace-filled expectations by following these four steps.

Developing Healthy Expectations – Step #1:
Make it Known

Known expectations are desires we have of a person or circumstance of which we are aware. For example, I have been taking out the trash for most of our marriage. It has been my designated chore. I recently had emergency surgery where I had to have part of my colon removed. This led to several weeks of recovery and limitations for how much I could lift. About four weeks into recovery, I noticed Lacey getting really frustrated at me. I wasn't sure why until she recognized the issue. She had been carrying the expectation that I would just naturally take out the trash when it was full like I usually did. I did not. It wasn't until she became frustrated and disappointed with me that she realized she was living with an unknown expectation.

Frustration or disappointment at a person (or situation) is often the only signal we have of an unknown expectation. Discovering this unknown expectation begins with acknowledging our frustration and disappointment. Thinking through what we hoped would have happened will reveal the unknown expectation. Releasing control of the desired outcome we hoped for through forgiveness will lead to us being free of the frustration and disappointment we feel. A known expectation — a desire we are aware of — is the first step in developing a valid expectation.

Developing Healthy Expectations – Step #2:
Make it Realistic

Realistic expectations are desires of a person or circumstance that are practical and reasonable. Lacey's expectation that I would take out the trash was technically a realistic one — I had been doing it for nearly 15 years. However, the difference was the major surgery. That made her realistic expectation an unrealistic one. The frustration and disappointment she felt toward me was because she was expecting me to do an unrealistic task while I was healing.

We become frustrated and disappointed when our expectations are not being met as a result of them being unrealistic. Clarification comes — and therefore a realistic expectation is developed — through communicating with the person and getting their feedback as to what is practical and reasonable. This is the second step in developing valid expectations.

Developing Healthy Expectations – Step #3: Make it Spoken

Spoken expectations are desires we voice and communicate with others. Lacey and I both laughed once she told me about her expectation of me taking out the trash. It was a ridiculous expectation.

Mutual frustration will be felt by both people when expectations are unspoken. This is often a result of believing *they should just know* or *it's obvious* about a need or desire we have. We need to identify and, if necessary, apologize for our unspoken expectation to resolve our frustration. Discussing, revisiting, and clarifying our expectations allows any unclear or unrealistic desires to be resolved. Lacey and I revisited the trash conversation once I started feeling better and could lift heavier weight. I began taking the trash out again... with some reminders from her. Defining, clarifying, and clearly communicating our desires to the other person validates the expectation. In some cases, writing out the agreed upon expectation may be necessary. This is the third step in developing a valid expectation.

Developing Healthy Expectations – Step #4: Make it Accepted

Accepted expectations are ones that the other person understands and agrees to. An expectation becomes invalid when someone does not agree to a conscious, realistic, and spoken expectation. Unaccepted expectations often come from the belief that someone *has to* or *needs to* do or say something (or not do or say something). This is especially true of people who hold specific roles in our life (i.e., parents, teachers, leaders, pastors, etc.) — we believe that just because they hold a title or position in our life, they should automatically fulfill the expectation that is accompanied by that role. Holding someone to an expectation they've not agreed to or are incapable of fulfilling only leads to unnecessary disappointment on our part and frustration on theirs. Re-evaluating and negotiating the expectation provides the opportunity to come to an agreement. An accepted expectation — one where both people involved agree to the terms — is the final step in making an expectation valid.

RESOLVING UNMET EXPECTATIONS

When Lacey and I were first married, it took me a while to recognize that taking out the trash was my chore. This became abundantly clear through Lacey's growing frustration and anger with me when I would forget to take it out. Unmet valid expectations are the healthy expectations we have of others that continue to go unfulfilled. This can often leave us feeling frustrated and disappointed. Left unresolved, these feelings breed bitterness and inhibit our ability to have a healthy relationship with the person. There are several steps we can take to resolve our valid disappointment and frustration.

Resolving Unmet Expectations – Step #1:
Forgive & Repent
For my marriage to be healthy, my wife and I had to forgive and apologize repeatedly to each other. This helped prevent the trash issue from becoming a bigger deal. Forgiving others for not meeting our valid expectations releases us from the stress and anxiety. Also, we may need to repent and apologize for judging them — and therefore responding poorly — for not fulfilling our

invalid expectations. If this does not resolve the unmet valid expectation, then perhaps clarity and negotiating the expectation needs to happen.

Resolving Unmet Expectations – Step #2: Clarify the Expectation

Misunderstandings of expectations should be communicated and clarified in a gracious manner — assuming the best about why they didn't fulfill the expectation. If the clarified expectation continues to go unmet, perhaps revisiting the expectation will bring it to a place of importance for the other person.

It took several conversations for me to embrace the fact that the trash was my chore. This also meant we had to clarify and agree to when the trash was actually "full."

Resolving Unmet Expectations – Step #3: Revisit the Expectation

Often, expectations are either forgotten or unconsciously ignored. Graciously revisiting and reminding the person of the expectation will prevent us from becoming frustrated. Lacey often had to remind me that I needed to take out the trash. Sometimes, she would put it in front of the door for me to take out as I left for work. I would unconsciously step over the trash on my way out. This was not a passive aggressive behavior. I literally didn't see it.

Resolving Unmet Expectations – Step #4: Negotiate the Expectation

If expectations continue to go unmet, we may need to graciously negotiate our expectations. Perhaps it's simply an issue of reasonableness. We may simply have too high an expectation — even if they agree to it — for them to fulfill it to our liking. Negotiating down to something that would be easier to achieve can minimize frustration and disappointment.

I'm ashamed to say that it often took Lacey starting a new bag of trash and setting it next to the full bag for me to get it. Lacey had grown tired of nagging me and I honestly didn't even see when it was full. I don't know what it was but seeing several bags piled up over the course of a few days bugged me enough to take it out.

Resolving Unmet Expectations – Step #5: Forgive the Expectation

If, after all the clarifying, reminding, and negotiating, the person still doesn't fulfill the valid expectation, we may need to simply forgive and release the expectation. Meaning, we release control of the desired outcome we have for a relationship or circumstance. For example: 1) this may mean releasing an employee from a job; or 2) releasing someone from a role or obligation you may justifiably expect of them, like a parent who is unwilling or unable to fulfill their responsibility. Either way, this means that we may need to fulfill the expectation ourselves or leave it unfulfilled to see who steps up and rises to the occasion. We must be careful to not pick up an offense from those who refuse to accept or repeatedly disregard our known, realistic, and spoken expectations.

Expectations for a circumstance are a little different. When something doesn't work out the way we planned or desired, there is often no one to forgive. Therefore, it is simply releasing control of what we would have liked to happen — allowing God's goodness to fix or redeem what was broken or unfulfilled. When we release control to Him, His Spirit brings peace and clarity to our mind regardless of the outcome. No matter what, we must trust that God is good and desires to work out the circumstance for our good.

———— // ————

Invalid expectations of others and our circumstances come from unhealthy assumptions. Ensuring that our expectations of others are known, realistic, spoken, and accepted will guard against frustration, disappointment, bitterness, and anger.

We also have to accept that circumstances may not always agree with our desires. We need to release our desire to control our circumstances — assuming and trusting that God is good and that He will work out our circumstance for our good. He will empower us through His Spirit to enjoy life no matter the outcome.

ACTIVATION STEP

Pray the following prayer. Be sure to take a few moments after you pray to silently wait for the Holy Spirit to respond. Then, write down what He says or shows you.

"Heavenly Father, thank You for caring for my unmet needs. Jesus, I know that having expectations of other people is not bad or wrong. I know that you want to help me resolve my frustration and disappointment with people. Holy Spirit, what person in my life am I frustrated or disappointed at because they have not lived up to my expectations for them?"

"Holy Spirit, what unmet expectation do I have of them?"

In the next few days, ask this person if they could get together with you to talk. If they agree to meet, go through the steps to resolving an unmet expectation. This may mean, if possible, that you first make the expectation a healthy one. Be sure to apologize to them if you have had any discouraging behavior toward them. Finally, if after several attempts at making your expectations of them healthy and they continue to go unmet, use *The Freedom Booklet* in the back of the book to work through your disappointment and frustration with them for not following through in fulfilling your expectations.

CHAPTER NINE

MURDER

EXTINGUISHING EXPLOSIVE OR SMOLDERING ANGER

Go ahead and be angry. You do well to be angry — but don't use your anger as fuel for revenge. And don't stay angry. Don't go to bed angry. Don't give the Devil that kind of foothold in your life.

— EPHESIANS 4:26-27, THE MESSAGE

I HONESTLY WONDERED IF MY WIFE WAS GOD'S PUNISHMENT TO ME BECAUSE OF MY ADDICTION.

I remember one day looking through Lacey's Bible early on in our marriage. I found the typical verse highlights and the notes one would usually find in a well-used Bible.

I continued perusing until I stumbled upon the Ten Commandments. Now, it's typical to find a commandment or two highlighted — often it's going to be the one that the Bible owner may struggle with the most. Popular commandments one may highlight usually are the ones concerning not committing adultery, not stealing, not taking the Lord's name in vain, or not lying or coveting. Oddly, none of the usual commands were highlighted in Lacey's Bible. The only one highlighted was, "You shall not murder."

I began to wonder, *Is this something she struggles with?*

If so, how often?

I jokingly asked her about it and she told me that it was for a study she had to do in her ministry school. We laughed about it and went on our way.

Murder may not have been an issue for her, but within the first couple years of our marriage, I began to realize she had a serious anger issue. I remember one argument we had where I told her that she was hurting my feelings. Without skipping a beat, she glibly responded, "How many more times do I have to hurt them before they die?"

As we began our third year of marriage, I honestly wondered if she was God's punishment for me as a consequence for my pornography addiction. Her anger terrified me — reminding me of my childhood with my dad. I believed this was my lot in life.

It took years for my wife to recognize where her anger and need to control came from. For her, it often led back to feeling uncared for or unheard. It was difficult for her to stop the immediate reactions — having to think through her words and behaviors. Over time, she developed new habits of pausing and listening. This chapter is based on what she discovered about the deep-rooted mindsets that led to her addiction to anger along with what she has learned in her freedom from it.

Healthy mindsets and behaviors affirm and strengthen how God created us physically, emotionally, mentally, and spiritually. Healthy behaviors are what the Bible calls righteousness.[1] The Holy Spirit will guide us to life-giving, de-escalating responses amidst conflict, disagreement, arguments, and in circumstances that make us feel out of control. Unhealthy behaviors do not credit God as the ultimate source of empowerment. These behaviors will almost always lead to escalating responses amidst an argument or disagreement — further compounding the issues in the conflict.

A healthy God-focused mindset motivates our behaviors based on the character and mission of God in our relationships. Conversely, an unhealthy mindset inhibits our ability to take into consideration His character, design, and plan for our lives. There are four different types of anger we can display with our mindsets and behaviors.

Anger Type #1:
Healthy Mindsets & Healthy Behaviors

This is the ultimate demonstration of healthy anger. This is where our motivation along with our words and actions are based

---

[1] See Acts 17:31; Romans 6:13; 8:5; Philippians 3:9; 1 Timothy 6:11

in the character and mission of the Heavenly Father. This anger benefits all people involved because it is directed by the Holy Spirit.

Anger Type #2:
Healthy Mindsets but Unhealthy Behaviors

Our motivations may be based in the Heavenly Father's character and mission. However, if our words, actions, or follow-through are not intentionally Spirit-led, our behaviors may cause further harm to an already painful situation. This anger is most likely going to be the most destructive for the people we were intending to help.

Anger Type #3:
Unhealthy Mindsets & Unhealthy Behaviors

This is the most obviously destructive form of a self-focused or self-serving anger. This is where both the motivation along with the words and actions used are self-gratifying and most often focused on revenge for the sake of "fairness." Ultimately, this anger is destructive for all people involved.

Anger Type #4:
Unhealthy Mindsets but Healthy Behaviors

This is perhaps the most deceptive form of anger as it appears right, moral, or even "Biblical." The behavior may be in line with God's character and mission, but it does not seek out the Holy Spirit's input and direction. This type of anger is often motivated by self-reliance and self-gratification. It can lead to a self-righteous or self-focused mindset. This form of anger can have devastating long-term effects on the person who is angry because of its self-sufficient nature. Since this anger is viewed as right and justified, the angry person is often unwilling to change. This judgmental type of anger can leave the person it is directed at feeling not good enough or powerless to change.

——————— // ———————

We demonstrate unhealthy anger — and reveal our selfish motivation — when we stand to gain anything from our anger. Unhealthy anger can reveal itself in two primary forms: smoldering anger and explosive anger. These forms of unhealthy anger are usually referred to as bitterness and anger respectively. These are unhealthy selfish internal (bitterness) and external (anger) reactions to specific offenses, hurts, or losses.

While we may genuinely "feel" bitter or angry, these reactions are usually our way of guarding or fighting against someone or something that has triggered a lie we have believed about our identity. These negative and often harmful reactions only perpetuate our pain, discomfort, and insecurity.

Our emotional reactions to conflict and uncomfortable circumstances are hard-wired into us during our early developmental years. These reactions are refined and solidified over time. Lacey grew up in a very loud, dramatic, and angry family. Throughout her life, people would often dismiss her anger as passion. Being "passionate" was normal for her. She recalls one story of talking to a mother who stated that they never yelled in their family. Lacey walked away from the conversation truly believing that the mother was a liar. It had become normal for Lacey to live in a world where everyone was loud and dramatic.

Unhealthy anger — whether explosive or smoldering — becomes the automatic negative reaction we habitually incline ourselves toward rather than stopping and listening for the Holy Spirit's leading.[2] Unhealthy anger becomes a self-gratifying and self-reliant way to fulfill a need or desire we have. These destructive behaviors lead to the death of relationships and ultimately, our own mind and emotions.

---

[2] See Psalm 37:8-9

Smoldering Anger

Smoldering anger is *a slow burning anger in our mind that produces an internal bitterness.* It is rooted in a steady vindictive mindset that often goes unnoticed.[3] Smoldering anger affects our perceptions of circumstances and people. As a result of these beliefs, our reactions become guarded, passive, and defensive — slowly killing our relationships.[4]

Explosive Anger

Explosive anger is *a quick burning anger in our mind that produces an external rage and temper.* It is rooted in an impatient and unstable mindset that is obvious and immediately destructive and self-gratifying.[5] As explosive anger spirals out of control, it negatively affects our relationships and exacerbates our negative circumstances. It becomes more aggressive, personal, and offensive as it loses control. These reactions quickly kill our relationships in an attempt to regain control through intimidation and manipulation.[6]

Whether our anger is internal or external, it is a reaction that we can have control over. The Holy Spirit will always guide us into

---

[3] See Hebrews 12:15
[4] See Genesis 4:3-8. Cain's anger was an internal bitterness that developed over time. He chose to kill his brother because he allowed this bitterness to build up in his mind. Bitterness killed his emotions, killed his thoughts, and ultimately killed his relationship with his brother when he killed him physically.
[5] See James 4:7-8
[6] See Exodus 2:11-12. Moses' anger was an immediate external reaction to seeing an Israelite — and his own identity — being mistreated by an Egyptian. He killed the Egyptian as his explosive anger overtook him. His explosive anger killed his emotions, killed his ability to think rationally, and ultimately killed his relationship with his people when he killed the Egyptian physically (Exodus 2:13-15).

a healthy way of expressing anger when we stop and listen for Him.[7] We can often use anger to either protect or fight against emotional, physical, or mental pain. Our unwillingness to release control of people and circumstances means that we allow ourselves to be controlled by negative emotions and offenses.[8]

Any mindset or reaction not rooted in God's character — trusting His goodness and love for us — will produce an unhealthy destructive anger. In Paul's letter to the churches in Rome, he writes that God's deepest desire is to make all circumstances and relationships work out for our good (Romans 8:26-29). This includes painful circumstances and the bad decisions people make that hurt us. While God does not intend or cause every painful situation, He is able to fix or redeem it for our benefit. When we release control, regardless of who or what brought the pain or offense into our lives, God has plans ready to make it better.[9] But, for His good plan to work, we need to release control of how we think it should work out.

HEALTHY ANGER

There were several occasions in Jesus life where he demonstrated healthy anger. These moments were motivated and empowered by the Holy Spirit.[10] By looking at these examples of Jesus' anger we can begin to understand the characteristics of healthy anger and the people or circumstances that necessitate it.

Jesus was Angry at Legalistic Church Leaders[11]

The Temple was a place where any person from anywhere in the world (both Jews and Gentiles) could come to pray and offer

---

[7] Genesis 4:6-7
[8] James 1:1-4
[9] Isaiah 54:14-17
[10] John 5:19, 30.
[11] See Matthew 21:12-13; Mark 11:15-19; Luke 19:45-47; John 2:13-22

sacrifices — a place to be reconciled with their Heavenly Father.[12] People would come from their respective nations with their unique currencies to purchase sacrifices. Originally, there was a system of money changers hired to arrange a system of fair exchange rates for the Temple currency. This money was used to buy the appropriate animals for the sacrifices and offerings. By the first century, the money changers had become corrupted by the priests who worked at the Temple.[13] They had inflated the exchange rate to a level that prevented people from buying their required sacrifices or voluntary offerings. Therefore, it was impossible for people from other countries to atone for their sins or offer gifts of thankfulness and generosity. Ultimately, this meant they were unable to be in right and healthy relationship with God.

> "These negative and often harmful reactions only perpetuate our pain, discomfort, and insecurity."

Because of this, Jesus became violent, throwing tables and chairs and whipping the temple workers and money changers. Jesus' violent anger was motivated by the Father's desire to have relationship with all people. His outward expression of anger was not for selfish gain, revenge, or self-gratifying. It was a physical demonstration of God's hatred toward the actions of those who hindered people from having relationship with Him — actions that make people believe that relationship with the Heavenly Father is difficult, expensive, or unachievable.

---

[12] Isaiah 56:6-8

[13] Pastor Mark Driscoll. "Angry Jesus Cleanses the Temple: The Temple's Taxes," Mars Hill Church, [Transcript], July 10, 2011, https://www.marshill.com/media/luke/angry-jesus-cleanses-the-temple; Updated link accessed August 27, 2020, http://www.realfaith.com/sermons/angry-jesus-cleanses-the-temple. See also, Alfred Edersheim, *The Life and Times of Jesus the Messiah.* (Hendrickson Publishers, 1993, vol. 1, 367-374.

Jesus was Angry at Legalistic People[14]

Jesus loved hanging out with parents and their children. They would often come to him to learn and for prayer and healing. They wanted to connect with him because they saw that Jesus was connected with the Father. One day while Jesus was teaching, several children got excited and ran up to him, knowing that Jesus enjoyed being with them. His disciples viewed this interruption as disrespectful, irreverent, and unmannered. They stepped in front of the children, blocking them from interrupting Jesus and yelling at them to stop. Because of the disciples' actions, Jesus became verbally angry with them.

This verbal reprimand had the same intensity as his physical rebuke in the temple.[15] Jesus' anger was once again motivated by his desire for relationship — the disciples were hindering children from having enjoyable relationship with him. They wrongly believed that a relationship with Jesus was only about serious learning and education rather than enjoying someone. Jesus knew that if the children felt like they could not be themselves around him, they would grow up believing God would not like who they were either. In rebuking his disciples, Jesus was laying a foundation of truth about who the Heavenly Father is — someone who is approachable, understanding, and enjoys silliness, laughter, and tickle-fights.

—————— // ——————

---

[14] See Matthew 19:13-15; Mark 10:13-16; Luke 18:15-17 (Matthew 18:1-14)

[15] The Greek word for "indignant" in Mark 10:14 is *aganakteo*. This word is the same word used for the anger of some of Jesus' disciples in Matthew 20:24; 26:8; Mark 10:41; 14:4 along with Jesus' enemies toward Him in Matthew 21:15; Luke 13:14. It is also the same word used in 2 Corinthians 7:11 for the "indignation" we are to have toward sin and its effects. These verses, in their context, reveal that being angry is not sinful but rather the motivation and means in which we express our anger can be.

There is always a deeper reason for our anger. If our motivation is self-serving, self-gratifying, or self-protecting our anger will always be unhealthy. This is why anger cannot simply be defined as an emotion. Jesus' anger did not claim any personal agenda. He was always motivated by his concern for people to have a healthy, enjoyable relationship with God. It was not selfish or self-seeking. The Holy Spirit motivated him to help reconnect people to the Heavenly Father who were being hindered by other people's useless rules or suffocating legalism.

OVERCOMING UNHEALTHY ANGER

Frustration have the same roots as anger, rage, and murder.[16] It is an attitude that demands *my way* results. This also includes any *my way* means by which we achieve these results. These frustrations, if not resolved through forgiveness, lead to unhealthy behavior. The following steps will help us live free of unhealthy anger.

Overcoming Unhealthy Anger – Step #1: Identify[17]

It is important to identify the root issue or cause of our frustrations. A while back Lacey was cleaning up our living room and had asked me to put away a DVD player we weren't using. She wanted me to put it on the top shelf of our closet. So, I placed it in a basket on that shelf, then I walked away. A few minutes later she came to me yelling because I had put the DVD player on top of a really nice vintage hat she had gotten in Europe. It was not a hat that was easily replaceable; however, I never saw it because it was at the bottom of the basket. After talking for a few minutes, she realized I did not mean any ill will toward her or her hat. She recognized her anger was actually rooted in feeling uncared for by me which triggered the anger.

---

[16] Ephesians 4:31-32; Colossians 3:8; James 4:1-3
[17] Matthew 6:14-15

If left unidentified — and therefore, unresolved — our frustrations lead to us reacting with unhealthy and unproductive anger that can hurt those we care about. These frustrations are often a result of unmet or invalid expectations, unfulfilled goals, or unexpected painful circumstances.

Overcoming Unhealthy Anger – Step #2: Release[18]

Our ability to forgive offenses will help us release control of our unmet goals or expectations that have caused us frustration and unhealthy anger. When I apologized to Lacey for making her feel uncared for, she forgave me. By this time in our marriage, she was able to recognize that possessions were not as important as having a healthy relationship. Over the years, this was something she had intentionally worked on. While her immediate reaction was one of anger, she had grown in her ability to move from that reaction to identifying the underlying feeling and forgiving me. A situation that would have lasted hours when we were first married took only minutes to resolve.

Our ability to release control of a person or situation can only come through trusting that God is good and desires good for us — even amidst painful, uncomfortable, or out of control situations.

Overcoming Unhealthy Anger – Step #3: Trust[19]

Often, we believe that we can only depend upon ourselves or others to fix, get through, or get over painful or uncomfortable circumstances. This independent or co-dependent mindset prevents us from receiving the Holy Spirit's peace and rest.

When Lacey forgave me, she chose to believe that my intentions toward her were not to make her feel uncared for. More importantly, she was choosing to trust the Holy Spirit to care for her when I did hurt her.

---

[18] Matthew 6:14-15
[19] Romans 8:28-29; James 1:2-4

Releasing control of what we think should happen and submitting our desires to the Holy Spirit's control allows us to receive His peace and rest into our mind — freeing us from anxiety, fear, and frustration.

Anger has often been defined as an emotion. However, the Scriptures point to **anger** being a behavior; that is, *our words and actions toward someone or something that has triggered a negative emotion or feeling in us* (Ephesians 4:26-32). Healthy anger is always motivated by love for both the person being hurt and the one doing the hurting. Its primary goal is for reconciliation with both God and people. Therefore, healthy anger will always be beneficial for others above what we can gain from it.

Healthy anger will require thoughtful planning and implementation; it will not be a momentary reaction. Responses are different from reactions in that a **reaction** is *something we do without thinking or planning;* it is often a habitual behavior we've learned and has become natural to us. A **response** is *a mindful decision we implement purposefully and strategically.* Healthy mindful responses can become natural reactions over time. But it does take time and intentionality for our responses to become reactions.

ACTIVATION STEP

Pray the following prayer. Be sure to take a few moments after you pray to silently wait for the Holy Spirit to respond. Then, write down what He says or shows you.

"Heavenly Father, thank You for helping me be free of unhealthy anger. Jesus, I trust that you are giving me healthy mindsets and behaviors that will lead to healthy anger. Holy Spirit, will You remind me about the last time I got angry at someone?"

"Holy Spirit, why did this person make me angry?"

In the next couple days, work through *The Freedom Booklet* in the back of this book for the person the Holy Spirit revealed to you. This can help you clarify your thoughts and feelings toward this person and what they did. Furthermore, the subject of anger is a great topic to invite someone in to be your *Encouragement Partner*. Once you fill out *The Freedom Booklet*, talk it through with your *Encouragement Partner*. They can help you develop a plan for how to deal with the feelings or unmet needs you discovered. They can also encourage you in the truths the Holy Spirit revealed to you at the end of *The Freedom Booklet*.

CHAPTER TEN

WRONG

THE HEALTHY NECESSITY
OF CONFRONTATION

But encourage each other every day while it is "today." Help each other so none of you will become hardened because sin has tricked you.

— HEBREWS 3:13, NEW CENTURY VERSION

I DIDN'T UNDERSTAND HOW MY WIFE COULD BE SO MEAN AND CRUEL TO ME WITH HER WORDS.

About seven years into our marriage, I felt had perfected the art of delivering a flawless sermon. In my mind, my sermons were the ideal balance of theology, doctrine, and cultural background. I studied between 15 to 20 hours a week in preparation to give the most eloquent one-hour sermon my audience would hear.

I perfectly defined the Greek and Hebrew verbs for my audience — giving them an understanding of how words were used in the original language. I painted with my words, a masterful background of historical and cultural facts about the passage on which I was speaking.

Most often the feedback was positive — people thanked me for opening their eyes and giving them new insight, wisdom, and revelation into the context and meaning of the Scriptures. I got the occasional heckler who would criticize my sermons — often only looking to debate a theological or doctrinal point. I welcomed these challenges because through the hundreds of hours I spent studying, I knew I would be proven right. And, more importantly, they would be proven wrong.

I remember a walk my wife and I went on one afternoon after giving one of my "world class" sermons. We were discussing details about the service — things we would change or improve — then we started talking about my sermon. I could tell she was holding back from sharing her thoughts, only giving me simple critiques and suggestions. I finally assured her that I welcomed her real thoughts, knowing she only wanted my best.

The next words that came out of her mouth will forever ring in my mind.

"Why does what you teach matter to me?" she asked.

I was shocked.

How could she ask me this in light of all the hours of study I had done?

How could she say this, knowing I had perfectly informed my audience of the context and background of the passage?

"Your ability to study theology and communicate that theology is great. You do a wonderful job. But why does that matter? Your sermons don't tell me why that particular theology or passage is important. There's no application or next step for your audience to walk away with," she explained.

I'll be honest, her words hurt me very deeply. It was like a punch to the gut that takes your breath away. I felt betrayed by my wife. I reflected upon the sermons I had given and realized the truth in her words. In a moment I concluded that the sermons I gave were truly meaningless — any hope, encouragement, or conviction that people experienced from those sermons was simply the grace of the Holy Spirit.

Lacey's willingness to confront me was incredibly difficult for both of us. Her vulnerability in sharing her thoughts and feelings opened her up to my defensiveness and backlash. And, her hard words made me feel like all my hours of study and perfecting my public speaking abilities were meaningless. However, it was one of the most beneficial confrontations I have experienced with my wife. Her ability to speak affirmation along with correction made the experience a positive one. Also, her well thought out arguments and desire for my good showed me how important this was to her.

It has forever changed the way I prepare a teaching. But more importantly, it has transformed the way I read the Bible — deepening the ongoing conversation I have with the Holy Spirit about what I am reading. I will often ask myself the question, *Why is what I am reading important — how does this apply to my life right now?*

———— // ————

Our Heavenly Father's heart for confrontation is always to bring life to all the people involved. Therefore, Spirit-led confrontation seeks and primarily desires good for the one being confronted. Often, our negative views of confrontation — something to avoid or something to always pursue — come from our experiences in our growing up years. We either mimic or reject what was modeled to us by our parents or caregivers.

The process of confrontation — either being confronted or being the confronter — should always begin by examining our own thoughts and motives, forgiving any offense and releasing any expectation we may have. Confrontation may never be perfect no matter who is involved. Therefore, in pursuing the best possible outcome for confrontation, we must always assume the best about the other person (either the confronter or the one we are confronting). This will guard against further offenses.

Confrontation must begin and end with humility. **Humility** is *agreeing with God for who we* (or another person) *are and what we* (or the other person) *can do.* A humble mindset does not believe less-than or greater-than thoughts about ourselves or others. It gives us courage and confidence when we feel confused, weak, or unsure — giving us clarity to hear the Holy Spirit's voice for the right words and tone. Humility also gives us strength and patience to remain silent and listen when we feel compelled to challenge someone. It allows the Holy Spirit's perspective and grace for the other person amidst a confrontation.

The writer of Hebrews challenges his readers, and us as well, to figure out ways to encourage and build people up daily (Hebrews 10:24-25). He urges us find unique ways to inspire people to live up to their God-given design. The idea behind this encouragement is confrontation — the positive reinforcement of their God-given identity and ability.

Unfortunately, we often view confrontation as a negative thing. We either try to avoid it (seeing it as unnecessary or unproductive) or we seek it out (hoping to be proven or affirmed as right). Both views are self-focused and self-gratifying — looking only to what is comfortable, good, and beneficial for oneself. They do not bring life to either person involved. Furthermore, neither view is founded upon a desire for life-giving interdependent relationship.

Unhealthy View: We Avoid Confrontation

This is my default, albeit unhealthy, view of confrontation. For most of my life, I avoided difficult conversations. Most of the time I simply didn't have the words to say or my brain couldn't process information fast enough to respond to people. Other times, I just didn't want to "stir the pot," so to speak.

Our desire to avoid confrontation is often based in fear of what other people may say or do. Avoiding confrontation can also minimize the need for truth to be known and justice to take place. Avoidance often leads to bitterness resulting in passive-aggressive behaviors. At best, it is ignoring or withdrawing from the situation to numb out or escape; at worst, it is ignoring or withdrawing from the relationship to avoid or punish the person.

This view may appear to be peaceful and gracious on the surface. However, it can be incredibly divisive and lead to grudge-holding, sarcasm, depression, anxiety, manipulation, isolation, jealousy, envy, gossip, and slander.[1]

Unhealthy View: We Seek Confrontation Out

This was my wife's default for many of the early years of our marriage. She needed to be right and affirmed as being right. Her genuine desire to have her thoughts and feelings validated led to a misguided view of confrontation. Rather than allowing me to hear her, she needed me to agree with her. Her insistence that agreement (especially with her) was the goal of confrontation meant that many of our fights ended with her demanding that I say or do something, and me becoming increasingly paralyzed.

---

[1] Proverbs 29:25; Matthew 10:28; 2 Corinthians 12:20; 1 Timothy 5:13

The desire to seek confrontation is often based in a need to be justified — focusing on being right in a matter rather than being in right relationship with someone. Paul writes in Ephesians 4:15 that we are to speak the truth in love. Unfortunately, people have used this verse justify their critical motivation. This passage is instead telling us that truth gives our love integrity and love makes this truth more attractive. Love sees and values people the same way God does; it creates an atmosphere where growth is encouraged.

Confrontation is the opportunity to speak truth about one's identity that is found in how God created them. It is not a license to be judgmental, critical, or unnecessarily harsh. This can often lead to anger and aggression — physically or verbally dominating a situation or conversation to control and manipulate it. This type of person often dominates a relationship by finding faults in the other person and thereby making themselves out to be right and justified in their criticisms.

Seeking confrontation may bring needed attention to a real issue. However, it can also be incredibly divisive and lead to blame, discouragement, unrealistic expectations of perfection, frustration, rage, nagging, criticism, lecturing, threatening hostility, and retaliation.[2]

STEPS TO HEALTHY CONFRONTATION

Confrontation is a necessary aspect of maturity and healthy relationships. Matthew 18:15-20 reveals God's design and intent for confrontation. His goal for difficult conversations is wholeness and growth, both for the individual and for the relationship. The following steps will lead to peace and resolution in your mind regardless of how the other person responds.

If more than one person is involved in a situation or another person is brought up in the conversation, it is important to hear

---

[2] Proverbs 14:29; 17:27; 29:22; 1 Timothy 5:13; James 1:19-20

both sides of an issue. I've often confronted one of my daughters about an issue to learn that it was the other one that was the instigator. Talking with both girls reveals details that help me determine how to accurately correct their behavior. Being able to talk with as many people directly affected by the situation as possible will bring a more complete view of the issue and each person's responsibility in a matter; it will help us more accurately confront the people involved.[3]

Healthy Confrontation – Step #1:
Examine Your Motivation

The first step in healthy confrontation is to allow the Holy Spirit access to our motives, expectations, and goals for the confrontation. He will reveal any unhealthy and unproductive mindsets that would hinder success in the confrontation. This may include any fault on our part (regardless of how big or small). Therefore, we may need to apologize and ask the person to forgive us before we can proceed with the confrontation.

Whether we are avoiding confrontation or seeking it, He may need to redirect our motives, convicting us toward healthy mindsets and expectations. This may require us to release control of our own desired goals of the confrontation — allowing Him the time and process needed to convict the other person. This will force us to re-examine our desires and "need" to confront. He will also give us strength and courage to confront — settling our minds and giving us clear thoughts and words when necessary.[4]

Healthy Confrontation – Step #2:
Forgive the Offender

To ensure the confrontation is truly for the benefit of the person we're confronting, we must forgive them for any hurt or

---

[3] Proverbs 18:2, 13, 15, 17 (1 Kings 3:16-28)
[4] Matthew 7:1-5

negative effects they may have caused us or those we love. This means we choose to release control of any expectations we have for how we believe they should respond. I highly recommend that before confronting you use *The Freedom Booklet* in the back of this book to help you forgive the person you desire to confront.

Releasing the person through forgiveness empowers us to live free of any negative reactions they may have to being confronted. Additionally, if we are avoiding a confrontation, forgiveness helps us truly desire the best for the other person. This healthy desire for the other person will overpower any fear or anxiety we may be experiencing.[5]

Healthy Confrontation – Step #3:
Assume & Desire the Best

Healthy, life-giving, hope-filled confrontation assumes God desires relationship with everyone. It sees every person, particularly those we need to confront, through the lens of being made in the image and likeness of God. Therefore, believing the best about the person helps us approach confrontation as a means of communication and clarification rather than a demoralizing personal attack. It affords them the opportunity to explain their mindsets, motivations, and behaviors.

Furthermore, desiring good for the person — their mental, emotional, physical, and spiritual well-being — is the foundation of healthy confrontation. Having the person's good in mind empowers us to confront them, especially if we would rather avoid the confrontation. Desiring good for them forces us to re-evaluate our motivation in our desire to confront. It may cause us to rethink our plan in what we were going to say or do. Assuming the best and desiring the best reveals our love for them above our own insecurities or desires.

---

[5] Ephesians 4:31-32

Healthy Confrontation – Step #4:
Confront Privately

We can begin planning our conversation only after we've completed the previous steps and believe a confrontation will be beneficial for the other person. This planning begins with an attitude of humility and grace. Furthermore, unless personal safety is an issue, this type of conversation should be done in private. This will prevent the other person from feeling shamed, embarrassed, or defensive.

Depending on the issue and your comfort level, this private conversation may go better in a public location — for example, a coffee shop or restaurant. If the issue is private, then I recommend a neutral location like a park. Your goal in choosing a public venue is not to make the issue public, but rather to provide a non-threatening location. Choosing a restaurant or coffee shop and offering to cover their food or drink will begin the conversation with a positive gesture. This offer is not meant to be a bait and switch; we must be upfront with them about our intentions for meeting. Beginning with a private conversation shows that we have their best interest in mind. The following steps will help bring clarity and goals to it:

a. **Apologize.** Our conversation with the person may require us to apologize and ask them to forgive us — refer to *Step 1: Examine Your Motivation*. Sometimes, we have played a role in the offensive behaviors of others. Either we were too harsh or expected too much, which led to their reacting offensively.

b. **Clarify.** Next, we need to be willing to clarify our understanding of what happened — telling them our thoughts, feelings, and perspective of the situation. Then, to be sure our understanding of the person's behavior and situation is accurate, we need to ask clarifying questions rather than start in with accusations.

c. **Confront.** Only after we clarify our perception of the other person's behaviors can we express our specific concerns. This is not a time to list out all our unresolved offenses with them. We are addressing one specific issue or concern we have with their mindset or behavior.

There are some phrases that will likely escalate the confrontation that we must try to avoid. The first type of phrase attacks the person's character with sweeping statements (e.g., "you always _____" or "you never _____"). The next type of phrase we must avoid distorts a person's identity with "you are" statements (e.g., "you're just a liar" or "you're an idiot"). Finally, another type of phrase we need to avoid assumes their motives are negative (e.g., "you're just saying that" or "you don't actually mean that"). These types of discouraging and discrediting phrases shame and invalidate the person's feelings and perspectives, making them defensive, aggressive, or withdrawn. Your goal is to make the person feel loved, heard, and cared for during the confrontation so they feel encouraged to make healthy changes. Attacking and demeaning their character, beliefs, or identity reveals our confrontation has become self-gratifying.[6]

d. **Contribute.** Before confronting the person, ask the Holy Spirit for ways the person could practically and specifically improve or correct their behavior. Without contributing some corrective ideas, your confrontation will only come off as critical, judgmental, and uncaring.

e. **Clarify… Again.** It would be good to, again, ask clarifying questions. This affirms our desire to understand and provides opportunity for them to restate their position. We need to hold loosely to our perceptions and hold firm to our commitment for understanding.

---

[6] Ephesians 4:29-32

f. **Release.** We should strive to help the other person by putting their needs above our own throughout the conversation and process of confrontation. The attitude of our motives and thoughts must be one of humility and grace. We may need to continually revisit forgiveness in our mind if the person responds negatively or unexpectedly. Forgiveness will keep in check our own responses toward them.

Furthermore, the person may never fully agree with our concerns or apologize to our satisfaction. This is where we need to release control of what we think should happen or how we think they should respond. Our unwillingness to release control will cause us to become aggressive and belligerent or passive and compliant.

> "God will honor our ability to humbly receive hurtful criticism — using it to our benefit, wholeness, and maturity."

Throughout the entire conversation we must be thoughtfully in prayer, seeking the Holy Spirit's direction during the conversation and when to end the confrontation.[7] Clarity, truth, and grace may come to the person only after the conversation has ended. Time may be needed in order for them to hear and respond to what the Holy Spirit is speaking to their mind.

One final note about allowing the Holy Spirit to convict is to offer encouragement before criticism. Recently, my daughter came in from outside and was huffing around the house. I was so tired of hearing her moan and have a bad attitude from earlier in the day

---

[7] Proverbs 18:8; 2:1-11

that I immediately sent her to her room. She responded quickly, yelling at me, "I only came in because I knew if I stayed out there, I would do something bad." She immediately began to cry as she stomped her way to her room. My wife looked at me with piercing eyes and said, "She did exactly what we tell her to do, to remove herself from the situation. You should have encouraged her with that rather than just lay into her about what she is doing wrong."

Encouragement is more than just sandwiching bad news; it speaks truth and life over the person from God's perspective. The Holy Spirit's conviction will be far more specific and beneficial for the person than a well-thought-out argument or criticism. But, we prepare a road for the Holy Spirit to bring specific conviction by affirming the steps they have already taken or by acknowledging a behavior we know they can possess when they allow the Holy Spirit to lead them. Speaking specific words of encouragement, grace, and hope over the person — although they may not yet be realized or perfectly demonstrated — allows the Holy Spirit to point out where their behavior is not meeting up with their God-given identity and ability.

For the record, I was wrong with my interaction with my daughter and I did apologize. I thanked her for removing herself from the situation, we talked about what she could do differently next time, and we worked out a plan for how she could change her general attitude. My wife's suggestion to encourage my daughter was far more successful than my original response.

Healthy Confrontation – Step #5:
Evaluate Your Expectations

Reconciliation (harmony within the relationship) can only take place when both forgiveness and repentance have been extended and received by all people involved. Furthermore, full restoration (trust rebuilt within the relationship) can only take place once the person has demonstrated mindset and behavioral changes over time. Full access (proximity) and trust may not always be possible.

Some relationships will take time for trust to be rebuilt and character to be reestablished. Healthy boundaries and caution for a time (or indefinitely) may be needed for safety and security. Recognizing what reconciliation and restoration are helps guard our mind from seeking invalid or unrealistic expectations of the person or relationship. Some relationships may never be restored or even reconciled simply because the other person is choosing unhealthy responses.[8]

Healthy Confrontation – Step #6:
Bring in a Mediator

In most cases, where two healthy, life-giving individuals are having a conflict, a private conversation is all that needs to take place for the relationship to be made whole. However, in some cases, a single conversation and giving the person time still isn't enough. We can feel like we need to have another discussion, or desire to withdraw from the relationship. In either case, we should revisit the first step: examining your motivation.

If you still feel like the Holy Spirit is asking you to further pursue another confrontation, it is healthy and wise to invite a neutral third-party into the conversation. This should be someone outside the situation or who has faithfully navigated and resolved similar situations in the past. Together, revisit the previous steps again, paying special attention to your attitudes, motivation, mindsets, and goals for the confrontation. Continue to assume the best and desire the best for the person. If, after this second conversation, you still feel like the person is not responding with healthy, life-giving, Spirit-led mindsets and behaviors then you may need to forgive and release control of the situation and person, including setting up boundaries. This does not mean you become cold or unapproachable to the person, but you diminish their access and influence in your life.

---

[8] 2 Corinthians 13:11; Galatians 6:1-5

If you and the person you're confronting are people who submit yourselves to a local church, and you feel the Holy Spirit prompting you to further confront the person, you have one last option. You can petition their church leadership to help you resolve the issue — making sure you walk through the first four steps of healthy confrontation with them.

If you or the individual are not a part of a local church community on a regular basis, this step is ill-advised. The lack of involvement and submission to a local church may reveal an unwillingness to receive wisdom, advice, or correction, or differing belief systems. At this point, simply forgive and release control of the person and their behaviors to God.[9]

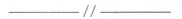

The steps of healthy confrontation laid out here may not apply to certain circumstances where safety and healthy boundaries are necessary. However, our willingness to forgive and release control of how we expect them to behave to will bring peace of mind and freedom from the painful thoughts and memories we have of the person. Freedom, peace, and hope are always possible for us when we forgive and release control to God whether the Holy Spirit directs us to confront or not to confront the person.

HOW TO RESPOND WHEN CONFRONTED

Most often, the Holy Spirit will use individuals to confront us about unhealthy mindsets and behaviors.[10] Second Samuel 12:1-15 gives us an example of how this looks. David, the king of Israel,

---

[9] 1 Corinthians 5:1-13
[10] 2 Chronicles 26:16-21; Jonah 3:1-10; Acts 5:1-11; Galatians 2:11-14

had an affair with another man's wife and then had her husband murdered. A few months later, David's friend, Nathan, came to him and told him a story about a man who had killed his neighbors beloved pet sheep to feed some guests. The injustice of the story made David so angry he wanted to seek out immediate retribution. Nathan clarified that the story was a metaphor about David. The beauty of this confrontation is that Nathan didn't come in immediately accusing David. He allowed David the opportunity to feel how his behavior had hurt others, then he brought up the issue that needed to be addressed. Because Nathan was able to get David emotionally invested before he confronted him, David had no other choice but to affirm that what he had done was wrong.

Unfortunately, the people who confront us may not have the best motivation or delivery methods as Nathan did with David. However, agreeing with God for our identity will enable us to receive imperfect confrontation. God honors our ability to humbly receive hurtful criticism and correction — using it to our benefit, wholeness, and maturity.[11]

Regardless of how we are confronted, there may be consequences to our misdeeds that we need to accept. Being forgiven does not always mean we are free of negative effects as a result of our misdeeds, ignorance, or immaturity.[12] Often these painful consequences help teach and direct us to make life-giving decisions in the future — helping us mature into healthy and whole people. These painful consequences may include broken trust in relationships, health issues, or civil and legal penalties. Scripture is clear that we are to trust God with people and His ability to deal with them.[13] When we lose trust with people because of our unhealthy behaviors, we need to earn it back through developing new healthy mindsets and behaviors. Beyond simply developing

---

[11] James 4:1-10; Philippians 2:1-11
[12] Numbers 5:5-8
[13] Jeremiah 17:5-8

these new habits, it may take more time for the other person to see and trust our new habits.

When confronted, an apology is the first step in righting a broken relationship. The following steps will help guide you in delivering a meaningful apology.

Response to Confrontation – Step #1:
Be Aware of Your Eyes & Tone

Face-to-face conversations always bring a deeper clarity and understanding that text or phone conversations simply do not. Consciously or not, seeing facial expressions and gestures help us interpret what someone is trying to communicate. Therefore, we should always seek to apologize in person. This will help communicate to the other person that the issue is important and worth the potential discomfort of having a face-to-face conversation. Furthermore, a sincere tone will communicate that you understand the gravity of the situation; empathizing with them will show them you understand the hurt you may have caused.

Response to Confrontation – Step #2:
Say, "I'm sorry for..."

We should be as specific as possible with our apology — expressing our regret for the behaviors that hurt or negatively affected the other person. Our apology should avoid generic statements like, "I was mean" or "I was hurtful"; it should acknowledge the specific words, actions, or tone (or lack thereof) that we believe to be the cause of the person's pain or offense.

There may be times when we did not intend or even know that we hurt someone. Asking the person to clarify specifically what we said or did that hurt them will help make our apology more precise. When confronted, whether we fully agree with what they said we did, we can apologize for causing them pain — affirming that it is never our goal to intentionally hurt them.

Response to Confrontation – Step #3:
Say, "This was wrong because..."

What we said or did and how it affected the other person should be the focus of the apology. When we begin to explain, defend, or justify our behavior, we diminish the other person's feelings — we invalidate and minimize our role in causing them pain. Furthermore, if we can acknowledge how we perceive our behaviors made the other person feel, it will help them feel loved, safe, heard, and cared for. For example, saying something like, "I see that when I said or did _____, it made you feel _____ (e.g., rejected, alone, disrespected, insignificant, used, etc."). For more examples of how someone might feel as a result of our behavior, review the list of feelings found in *Step 2: Attitudes, Thoughts, Beliefs, & Feelings* of *The Freedom Booklet* located in the back of this book.

Response to Confrontation – Step #4:
Say, "In the future, I will..."

Planning our next response and communicating this plan with the other person will help rebuild trust. This will show them that we have put time and energy into how we might change our behavior. But, simply talking about this plan without implementing it will only make us untrustworthy. Therefore, our plans need to be realistic with our abilities and not just hopeful desires. Actually doing what we said will show them we're committed to rebuilding the relationship.

Response to Confrontation – Step #5:
Ask, "Will you forgive me for..."

Finally, we need to ask them to forgive us for the specific behavior that caused pain or affected them negatively. For example we might ask them, "Will you forgive me for _____?" Being specific about our hurtful behavior will provide them the opportunity to be free of the offense through forgiveness. I remember one time a ministry leader I worked with said something negative toward me in a team meeting. After the meeting before everyone left, she apologized to me and asked me to forgive her. I flippantly responded with, "It's okay." After the third time apologizing and asking me to forgive her, I finally said, "Yes, I forgive you." This exchange taught me the importance of valuing the weight of an offense. The Holy Spirit had deeply convicted her, and my dismissal of her apology devalued that conviction. Furthermore, by dismissing her apology, I was not valuing the effects her words had on me.

Unfortunately for some people, no amount of apologizing or restitution will satisfy a person's expectations or demands for retribution. Nothing we say and do will be enough for them to truly forgive us. This is where our confidence in our God-given identity will help us remain free of their unrealistic expectations. Our ability to receive the Father's forgiveness and build new behaviors will guard us from being hurt by their unwillingness to forgive us.

Confronting someone is rarely ever easy and will, more than likely, be incredibly messy. However, when we avoid or reject confrontation, we deny the person an opportunity to grow and mature. This is often because we are more concerned about our own comfort and well-being than we are for what is good for the other person. Conversely, our desire to be heard or understood can often lead to us intimidating, manipulating, or controlling the person rather than caring for them. Both of these views of confrontation are deeply self-serving. This is why we must listen for the Holy Spirit's direction in confrontation. Ultimately, healthy confrontation cares for the other person's good above our own desires and is necessary for healthy relationships.

ACTIVATION STEP

Pray the following prayer. Be sure to take a few moments after you pray to silently wait for the Holy Spirit to respond. Then, write down what He says or shows you.

"Heavenly Father, thank You for Your grace and mercy. I know that I may not have confronted people in a healthy way in the past. I choose to receive Your forgiveness for [seeking out/avoiding] people about difficult issues."

"Holy Spirit, who is someone You are directing me to confront about an unhealthy attitude or behavior in their life?"

"Holy Spirit, what specific words or actions can I say or do to help confront this person in a way that will encourage them, comfort them, and build them up?"

"Holy Spirit, who is someone You are asking me to trust You with by not confronting them?"

"Holy Spirit, what specific words or actions can I say or do to encourage, comfort, and build up this person without having to confront them?"

In the next few days, follow through with confronting and encouraging the people the Holy Spirit directed you toward. Be sure to forgive and release control of their behaviors by revisiting and working through *The Freedom Booklet* in the back of this book.

Be intentional about setting up time to talk with each person — one with the goal of confrontation and the other with the goal of encouragement.

For the person the Holy Spirit led you to confront, be sure to follow the previously mentioned steps for healthy confrontation.

CHAPTER ELEVEN

MESSY

RECOVERING PEACE IN
YOUR RELATIONSHIPS

All this comes from the God who
settled the relationship between us and
him, and then called us to settle our
relationships with each other.

— 2 CORINTHIANS 5:18, THE MESSAGE

HER ATTEMPT FOR RECONCILIATION
WAS MESSY AND LACKED FINESSE.

We adopted our second daughter from birth. She has not known a home other than ours. However, her knowledge of being adopted has led to unique responses to us disciplining her.

Lately, her go-to response to our "unfairness" as parents is demanding we send her back to her "real" family. This is often followed up with a long monologue about how her "real" mom and dad wouldn't treat her this way and how awful this family treats her.

Recently, one of these rants was squarely directed at me. All her frustration came out in a string of disparaging accusations toward me and what she believed I thought about her. Once she had a night to sleep on it, she woke up and decided to make me — the person she believes does not treat her fairly — breakfast. The scrambled eggs were runny and since we were out of my favorite breakfast food (cottage cheese) she made me a bowl of sour cream. Her attempts for reconciliation were messy and lacked finesse. However, her desire for our relationship to be made right was flawless. She felt genuine remorse for what she had said about me.

For our relationship to be reconciled my expectations of her (and what she was capable to bring to the relationship) needed to be what she was able to live up to. I could have focused on how horrible the breakfast was — the eggs were practically raw, and who doesn't know the difference between cottage cheese and sour cream? But I chose to focus on her heart and the effort in her attempt to show love toward me.

Apologies, whether our own or someone else's, will rarely be perfect. In fact, the apology may come off as more offensive then the original offense. However, our ability to focus on their intent and desire for relationship over their words and actions will guard us from further offense.

———— // ————

The Heavenly Father has already extended forgiveness toward everyone through Jesus.[1]   It is our willingness to receive His forgiveness that determines our repentance.[2]   Therefore, it is in receiving God's forgiveness coupled with our repentance that reunites us, bringing peace and harmony to our relationship. It is this example of how our relationship with God is reconciled that we define resolution within our human conflicts. An offending person has the choice to not repent or receive our forgiveness. Similarly, when we apologize and repent, they can choose to not forgive us.

Too often we can sacrifice God's peace within a relationship because we can have a wrong or incomplete view of reconciliation. Striving toward peace within our relationships with this distorted view of reconciliation only produces discouragement, frustration, and disappointment.

Reconciliation is *the establishment of peace and harmony back into a relationship through the means of forgiveness and repentance.* Forgiveness is extended by the offended and received by the offender. Repentance is extended by the offender (often accompanied by a genuine apology) and is accepted by the offended.

Unfortunately, reconciliation may not always be possible if either person is unwilling or unable (due to distance or death) to forgive or repent. It is further complicated if ownership for each person's part in the conflict is not accepted.   Additionally, the expectations we have for how the other person should behave in the relationship can further hinder reconciliation from happening.

Despite whether reconciliation takes place, we can always have resolution and peace of mind when we do what the Holy Spirit asks

[1] 2 Corinthians 5:11-6:1
[2] Colossians 1:19-23

us to do, regardless of the other person's response.[3] While we have a responsibility, as far as it depends upon us, to pursue peace and harmony with others[4] we are not responsible for their reactions. However, our words and behaviors toward them amidst conflict can be encouraging (blessing) or discouraging (cursing).[5] It can affect their view of themselves and therefore impact their perception of how God views them. Therefore, a person's ability to have a healthy, vibrant relationship with God (and how they respond to us) can be affected by our interactions with them.

WHEN TO ASK FOR FORGIVENESS

The author of Matthew once recalled a time when Jesus spoke about when to ask someone for forgiveness (Matthew 5:21-26). Jesus said that pursuing reconciliation with someone was more important to the Heavenly Father than our participation in the local church. Therefore, our financial generosity, attendance, worship, Bible study or small group participation are all rendered meaningless when we know that we've offended someone and are unwilling to reconcile with them.

We can intentionally or unintentionally hurt people in two ways: by the things we say and do and by the things we don't say and do. The hurt we cause others is often referred to as "sinning against them."[6] While unintentional misdeeds don't often carry the same consequences as the ones we intentionally commit against others,[7] the pain we cause them is real and can be just as deep.

The things we say and do (or **misdeeds of commission**) are *any attitudes, thoughts, actions, words, or motivations that we have toward people that are not in line with God's character, design, or plan.* These are

---

[3] Luke 17:3-4
[4] Romans 12:18
[5] James 3:1-12
[6] See Matthew 18:15, 21; Luke 17:4; 1 Corinthians 8:12
[7] 1 John 5:16-17

often seen in our behaviors or beliefs that we have of people. This includes the negative or belittling things we say to or about people, our negative assumptions about them, and our discouraging or hurtful actions we take toward them.

The things we don't say and do (or **misdeeds of omission**) are *any attitudes, thoughts, actions, words, or motivations that we do not have toward people that are in line with God's character, design, or plan.* These are often displayed by our unwillingness to confront, talk, or act in a way that may be beneficial for someone. Neglecting a responsibility or commitment we have toward someone can also cause pain. This abandonment can include not supporting someone, not listening or speaking to someone, or not taking an active role in someone's life (e.g., speaking words or taking actions of care and love toward them).

One final way we commit sins of omission is in our unwillingness to believe, think, or do something the Holy Spirit has asked us to do.[8] Hurting the people around us often stems from our mistrust or distrust of God. This lack of reliance upon Him will cause us to ignore and diminish His voice in our mind. We will feel out of control as we disregard His guidance and direction. Unfortunately, this causes us to have unhealthy behaviors that hurt others while we continue to hurt ourselves.

When we hurt people or do things that cause them emotional, physical, or mental pain, we should seek forgiveness from both the person we hurt and from God (for breaking His heart by hurting His creation). The following are reasons we may need to seek forgiveness from the person we hurt.

Ask for Forgiveness When:
We Agree that We Have Hurt the Person

Depending on what we did, it can be difficult to admit we've hurt someone. It can bring about feelings of shame, guilt, and fear.

---

[8] James 4:17; see also Luke 12:47-48

However, for us to be free from this hurtful behavior, we must seek forgiveness from the person we wronged. Furthermore, we must trust and receive the forgiveness that the Heavenly Father has already extended toward us.

As we have previously stated in this book, we may learn of our hurtful behavior through the person we hurt, another person, or directly from the Holy Spirit. Whatever the case may be, we must apologize and, if possible, compensate the person for the damage we caused.

Ask for Forgiveness When:
We Don't Think We're Wrong

We may need to seek forgiveness even if we don't agree that we were wrong or offensive in our behaviors toward another person. Apologizing and seeking forgiveness for hurting someone does not mean that we were wrong or intentionally did something malicious. It simply acknowledges and affirms the person's feelings and how they perceived our behavior. In fact, Jesus, in Matthew 5:23-24, does not give us the option to apologize and seek forgiveness only when we agree with their feelings. He simply says to go and make it right with the person who is offended at us.

Feelings are neither right nor wrong, therefore when we affirm a person's feelings, we show them that we value them more than being right. I remember one argument Lacey and I had when I didn't say one word. However, she was offended by me and stormed off to our bedroom. I remember sitting in our living room thinking to myself, *What just happened? What did I do? I literally said nothing.* It was at this last statement that I felt the Holy Spirit nudging me by saying, "Exactly." I realized in that moment that my silence and desire to avoid conflict made her feel uncared for. I thought for a moment about what I was going to say then went to her to apologize for not valuing her feelings and affirming her.

Seeking forgiveness from an offended person gives them the opportunity to clarify their thoughts and share their perspective.

Often, is only when we seek forgiveness for our part of a conflict that we can have peace within the relationship.

Ask for Forgiveness When:
Restitution is Needed

Sometimes our behaviors require us to pay back what we can. For example, in the case of stolen or destroyed property, we may need to return the property or make restitution.[9] In other cases, if the offense is something we've said, restitution may be saying a kind, heartfelt compliment to the person. Another way to pay restitution is by observing what makes the person feel cared for or loved, and then doing that thing. This means we may have to spend quality time with the person, speak or write encouraging words to them, serve them in a meaningful way, or for some, it may be as simple as a hug and looking them in the eyes when we apologize.

Regardless of what the offense may have been, true remorse desires to make right what was wronged. It attempts, as far as it is reasonable, to make amends by providing compensation or correcting what was done.

Ask for Forgiveness When:
We Are Convicted

In some instances, we may never see the negative effects of our behavior on others. The Holy Spirit will be faithful in revealing who we hurt and how we hurt them. He may also convict us of a wrong we've done even if the other person wasn't offended. During my time of teaching at a Bible school, I once had a student apologize to me and ask me to forgive her for a sarcastic comment she had made. I remembered the conversation and we were both making our fair share of sarcastic comments. I wasn't offended in the slightest; however, the Holy Spirit convicted her that she was wrong and needed to apologize.

---

[9] Luke 19:2-10

We may not always agree with God when He convicts us — especially if what we did or said was correct, accurate, or right. While our behavior may be justified by our perception of the events, the motives, thoughts, or beliefs behind our words or actions may not have been healthy or beneficial.

First John 1:9 reveals that freedom and peace can only come when we confess our misdeeds to God and receive His forgiveness. There are instances when we may not need to seek forgiveness from a person. The following examples are just that, examples. As always, we need to remain attentive to the Holy Spirit for His guidance and leading.

We May Not Need to Seek Forgiveness When:
Our Offense is a Thought or Motive

These are unhealthy thoughts that do not take the form of words or behaviors. Jealousy, unacted upon anger, sexual lust, etc., are all examples of unhealthy thoughts that may not necessarily affect another person; therefore, it may be unnecessary or even detrimental if we do apologize. While these unhealthy thoughts do affect our own well-being, they are only known to us and God. However, by confessing them to a trusted, Spirit-led person (i.e., an *Encouragement Partner*), we invite their support in our efforts toward wholeness. They can help us develop a plan to overcome these thought patterns and encourage us toward freedom.

We May Not Need to Seek Forgiveness When: We've Offended a Repeat Offendee

Some people have victim mindsets — they have a pattern of being offended and often enter relationships and circumstances expecting to be hurt, failed, or disappointed. Because of their own unresolved pain, they will never be content with any level of remorse or restitution. They are perpetually unwilling to forgive and are never satisfied by any amount of payback.

We May Not Need to Seek Forgiveness When: We're Willing but Unable to Apologize

We may be fully willing and ready to seek forgiveness, apologize, and make restitution for our hurtful behavior, but due to death or distance we may not be able to do so. In these instances, having a desire to walk in the spirit of Matthew 5:23-24 can be sufficient. This inability to resolve the issue with the person can result in unnecessary guilt, shame, and condemnation — we can be free and whole.

For us to have peace, it is vital that we trust and receive the forgiveness God has for us and guard ourselves from untrue or defamatory thoughts about ourselves. We need to be attentive and aware of our thoughts, receiving God's truth about how He views us rather than how someone else might view us in light of the unresolved issue.

THE PROCESS OF SEEKING FORGIVENESS

Seeking forgiveness desires the best for the person we've hurt. Therefore, there are several steps we can take to ensure that we are caring for the other person as we seek to be forgiven. While choosing to forgive is their choice, we want to be sure we've taken every reasonable effort to make them feel cared for and heard.

Seeking Forgiveness – Step #1:
Forgive, If Applicable

Before we seek to be forgiven, we must be sure to forgive the other person of any part they may have played in the conflict. This will ensure our apology is not motivated by our desire to get something from the person. While seeking forgiveness can free us from an offense, it should only be motivated by our desire to care for and love the person we have hurt or offended.

Seeking Forgiveness – Step #2:
Clarify the Offense

Fully understanding the effects our behavior has on someone may not be possible without further conversation with the person. However, we need to define the offense to the best of our knowledge before we move to step three. Asking the Holy Spirit to bring clarity and understanding will help in this process.

Seeking Forgiveness – Step #3:
Receive the Father's Forgiveness

We can often look at our hurtful behaviors as not truly affecting the heart of our Heavenly Father. However, from His perspective, our actions have caused people pain — His children have suffered because of our words and actions. Furthermore, our unhealthy mindsets and behaviors can bring pain and suffering to ourselves — something He never desires for us.

For us to live in the Holy Spirit's peace and confidence, we need to receive the Father's forgiveness for choosing to believe and behave in hurtful ways toward others and ourselves. Confessing these mindsets and behaviors to Him and apologizing for them (out loud if possible) is a catalyst for our repentance. Finally, trusting and receiving His forgiveness frees us from shame, guilt, and condemnation. I thoroughly discuss this in *The Freedom Booklet* at the back of this book. Go through this resource as you being the offender. Pay special attention to *Step 9: Receiving and Replacing*.

Seeking Forgiveness – Step #4:
Seek Understanding

True clarity and understanding of how our behavior affected someone may only come once we have a conversation with the offended person. In seeking understanding, we need to be careful not to minimize, justify, excuse, or defend our words or actions — we need to admit our behavior was hurtful.

> "The inability for a relationship to be restored does not negate our responsibility to forgive."

One issue we can have in clarifying the offense is that it can become over complicated and confusing. This is where asking the Holy Spirit to bring clarity and understanding is beneficial. Ask the person if they would be willing to pray with you in seeking understanding from God. Then as you're talking, be sure to stay on subject and not allow distractions or other circumstances or events to be brought into the conversation.

Seeking understanding and clarity is not a time to confront or bring up unresolved offenses toward the person. Asking for forgiveness is our time to acknowledge, confess, and apologize for our hurtful attitude and behavior.

Seeking Forgiveness – Step #5:
Ask for Forgiveness

We need to be clear in what we are asking from the other person. In the previous chapter I broke down in detail what a healthy apology looks like. In short, we may say, "I see that when I [insert your behavior] it made you feel [insert their emotion]. Will you forgive me for [insert your behavior]?"

Asking clarifying questions can help us identify, acknowledge, and affirm the person's feelings. This will also help us know how to accurately ask for forgiveness.

Similar to confronting someone, one thing to keep in mind is when, where, and how we seek forgiveness. The timing, location, body language, and tone of voice can make all the difference in their response. This includes incorporating some of the restitution examples I previously listed.

Lastly, if possible and depending on what we said or did, seek advice from the one we offended. Asking them how our attitude or behavior could be better next time takes humility on our part, but it goes a long way in defusing their anger and frustration. While we may not completely agree with their solution, it can bring revelation to an issue we are unaware of and encourage us to build new, Spirit-led attitudes and behaviors.

HOW TO BUILD HEALTHY BEHAVIORS

As we pursue forgiveness from others, it is important that we also pursue building new, healthy mindsets and behaviors. The sincerity of our remorse and apology will be revealed by our change of mind and life. One step beyond reconciliation is the restoration of a relationship. **Restoration** is *giving full access and trust to the offending person — leading to a healthy, life-giving, Spirit-led interdependent relationship.* This is where vulnerability and intimacy are reinstated. In chapter six we saw that repentance is new mindsets proven over time through new behaviors. This proven repentance needs to take place before a relationship can be restored. Believing that a relationship isn't reconciled until we can trust the offending person is confusing restoration with reconciliation and can lead to frustration or disappointment. Similarly, trying to restore a relationship before the person demonstrates proven repentance will lead to disappointment and frustration. The inability for a relationship to be restored does not negate, however, our responsibility to forgive; forgiveness and peace are always possible despite the actions and behaviors of other people.

Desiring to restore a relationship as the offending person means we strive to reasonably prove our repentance. Through the course of our life we have taken the time and effort to cultivate bad habits (neural connections and chemical bonds within our brains) that led to unhealthy mindsets and behaviors; essentially, we addicted ourselves to unhealthy desires that led to unhealthy behaviors. This means it takes a greater amount of effort and reliance upon the Holy Spirit to develop new, healthy desires. These new desires renew our mind and create healthy Spirit-led behaviors. As we live from these healthy mindsets and behaviors our repentance is revealed. Our old ways of thinking and behaving will fade away.

While a miracle (an instant change of desire or behavior) is possible, God often uses process and time to change us. Paul wrote to the church in Colossae that their old ways of thinking and behaving are being gradually changed into what God originally designed for them (Colossians 3:9-10).[10] The following is the process for building new, Spirit-led mindsets and behaviors.

Building Healthy Behaviors – Step #1:
Be Vulnerable and Transparent

Exposing our temptations and weaknesses to a trusted, Spirit-led friend or family member invites grace and support. This

---

[10] See also Romans 12:2. In the ESV translation, Colossians 3:9 reads, "put off the old self with its practices". The idea Paul is conveying in Colossians 3:9-11 is that our old way of viewing ourselves (our habitual mindsets and beliefs) along with our behaviors (our habitual attitudes and habits) are being changed. He uses the verbiage of an actor taking off his character costumes. Our nature (having been made in the image and likeness of God) is not affected by our "old self" (our character costumes). Rather, the "new self" is us putting on our "normal clothes" — living in agreement to who we really are; that is, in line with who God created us to be.

Encouragement Partner empowers us to overcome temptations or unhealthy desires. Unfortunately, the things we desire most to keep secret or private will be our greatest area of struggle.[11] Living connected and vulnerable helps us fight shame and therefore overcome unhealthy mindsets and behaviors. Our *Encouragement Partner* can help us develop a plan for overcoming our weaknesses by developing new mindsets and behaviors.[12]

Building Healthy Behaviors – Step #2:
Live Listening to the Holy Spirit

The Holy Spirit always leads us into life-giving mindsets and behaviors. These are encouraged through connection with other Spirit-led friends and family. As the Holy Spirit has access to more of our mind and life, we naturally begin to have healthy mindsets and behaviors.[13]

Building Healthy Behaviors – Step #3:
Replace the Lies with Truth

Regardless of our behaviors or what we believe about ourselves, we must affirm and agree with God for our identity; specifically that we are created in His image and likeness. As we trust the Holy Spirit, we become more than conquerors over temptation, weakness, failure, sin, and mistakes. The fullness of God will live in us; His Spirit that raised Jesus from the dead will empower us. Because we have the Holy Spirit living in us, we have the same mind, desires, and thoughts as Jesus. Affirming our God-given identity and Spirit-led abilities will encourage healthy mindsets and behaviors. We become confident in who God created us to be and this mindset impacts what we do (i.e., live free of sin[14]).

---

[11] Job 24:13; John 3:16-21; Romans 13:12; Ephesians 5:11-13
[12] See 1 Thessalonians 2:13; 5:14; Hebrews 10:25
[13] See Romans 8:4; 12:2; 2 Corinthians 4:16; Galatians 5:16, 25; Ephesians 4:23
[14] See Psalm 1:1-2; 77:12; 119:15; Romans 6:11; 8:11, 37; 12:2; 1 Corinthians 2:16; Ephesians 2:10; 4:23-24; Philippians 4:8; Revelation 12:1

Building Healthy Behaviors – Step #4:
Reward Yourself

God created our brains to seek out and receive rewards through chemical transmitters. Into Action Recovery Center (IARC) states on their website that dopamine is one of the "feel good" chemicals in our brain. Dopamine — along with other chemicals like serotonin, oxytocin, and endorphins — interacts with the pleasure and reward center of our brain. Essentially, these "reward" chemicals affect how happy we feel. Dopamine can also affect our movement, memory, and focus.[15]   Therefore, these chemical "rewards" help us build healthy habits and connections by driving us to seek out and repeat pleasurable activities and experiences.

I hate running. So when my doctor told me that I had to incorporate cardio exercises into my daily routine, I knew I would have to be creative with how I would reward myself. When I started going to the gym I decided to go when my favorite radio program was airing. This gave me the incentive I needed to start running.

Recently my daughter got in trouble for lying to her friends. When I asked her about it, she immediately owned up to the lie — something she would usually try to hide or justify. While she did have consequences for lying, I later rewarded her for being honest.

Whatever it is we are trying to change or accomplish, it is always easier when we build in a reward system. Whether it's starting an exercise routine, having to have a difficult conversation with someone, or quitting an unhealthy behavior, these rewards become our motivating factor. A friend of mine recently told me that when the Holy Spirit prompted her to have weekly meetings with someone who was difficult to talk with, she decided to meet them

---

[15] "Effects of Dopamine: How Dopamine Drives Human Behavior," Into Action Recovery Center, accessed May 29, 2020, https://www.intoactionrecovery.com/how-dopamine-drives-our-behavior/. See also, Schultz W (July 2015). "Neuronal Reward and Decision Signals: From Theories to Data"; Robinson TE, Berridge KC (1993). "The neural basis of drug craving: an incentive-sensitization theory of addiction"; and Wright JS, Panksepp J (2012). "An evolutionary framework to understand foraging, wanting, and desire: the neuropsychology of the SEEKING system"

at her favorite coffee shop. Looking forward to having a good cup of coffee gave her the initial boost she needed to overcome the hesitancy she felt in meeting with this person. Rewards give us the positive feelings and emotions we sometimes require to begin the healthy, Spirit-led behaviors we need to build.[16]

Building Healthy Behaviors – Step #5: Give Yourself Time

Except in the case of a miracle, habits will take time and energy to form. If you've been doing something for 15 years, you can expect it to take more than a few hours or even days to overcome that behavior. Or, conversely, if you need to start doing something that seems foreign to you, it will take time to feel comfortable doing that thing. For example, if expressing your feelings or thoughts is uncomfortable for you, it will take time and practice for you to feel comfortable opening-up and being vulnerable.

I grew up in a quiet home where sharing our thoughts and feelings was not normal. So, when Lacey was working with me on sharing my feelings it was beyond difficult. We started with a journal — this gave me the space and time needed to develop my thoughts and then communicate them in an understandable way. When I was finally able to verbally share my feelings, Lacey had to learn how to stop and listen. The family she grew up in was loud and dramatic. Therefore, it took her a while to learn how to not shut me down by immediately responding.

Developing new mindsets and behaviors requires patience, consistency, and intentionality. God designed our brains in such a way that it takes at least 40 days for a new behavior to feel comfortable and natural. We need to give ourselves grace as God gives us grace to build new mindsets and behaviors.

---

[16] See Matthew 6:4; Luke 6:35; Colossians 3:24; Hebrews 10:35; 11:6; 2 John 8

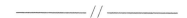

Asking someone to forgive us can be humiliating, difficult, and produce feelings of shame. But for us to be reconciled with the person we've offended (and have the same trust and access into their life we once had) we must be willing to ask them to forgive us. It provides a foundation of honesty and vulnerability that makes a relationship stronger.

The offended person may never forgive us. However, this is not our responsibility. Remembering that reconciliation takes both repentance *and* forgiveness will guard our mind against frustration and disappointment. Getting stuck by someone's unwillingness to forgive us will only fuel our pain and perpetuate our unhealthy behaviors. When we recognize ourselves becoming offended by their unwillingness to forgive, we must walk through the process of forgiveness ourselves.

Peace in our mind and life is always possible despite the status of a relationship. However, the extent to which we experience this peace depends upon our willingness to listen and trust the Holy Spirit in guiding us toward wholeness. We can be confident that our relationship with the Heavenly Father is reconciled when we agree with and receive His forgiveness for our misdeeds. Releasing control of the person and their response to God will free us from anxiety, fear, and the need to control.

ACTIVATION STEP

Pray the following prayer. Be sure to take a few moments after you pray to silently wait for the Holy Spirit to respond. Then write down what He says or shows you.

"Heavenly Father, thank You for Your patience and support. I know that You desire wholeness and peace in my mind and life. I choose to trust that You are good and have good for me even when You reveal thoughts and behaviors that are not healthy or in line with how You created me."

"Holy Spirit, who have I had unhealthy or hurtful thoughts or behaviors toward?"

"Holy Spirit, what specific thoughts, words, or actions have I had toward them that have been unhealthy or hurtful?"

"Holy Spirit, I ask that you help me make things right between me and this person. I ask that you give me favor and wisdom as I seek forgiveness from them."

In the next few days, follow through with the process of seeking forgiveness from this person. Be intentional about setting up time to talk with them and, if possible, making reasonable restitution.

YOU ARE AND YOU WILL BE...

(the conclusion)

I WAS A DRUMMER... BUT I DIDN'T KNOW HOW TO PLAY THE DRUMS.

My dad was a pastor while I was growing up. Our house was the parsonage — the house owned by the church but usually reserved for the pastor and his family. When I was about eight years old, I began going to the church after school to practice the drums. I would play over the loudspeakers whatever CD's I had at the time. From early Christian rock bands like Petra or White Heart to Britney Spears, Blink-182, or Aerosmith, I would bang away at those drums. Over the course of several years, and updating my CD playlist, I became proficient. I even started playing the drums for our church.

Since some of my friends attended different churches, I would go with them to their youth groups. Inevitably I ended up playing in their youth group worship bands. I became hesitantly optimistic in my abilities and regularly referred to myself as a drummer. That is, until I tried out to be the drummer for one of the larger youth groups in our city.

I had made it past the tryout, but when I showed up for practice on the night I was supposed to play, they introduced a song that had a 3/4 time signature. I, however, only knew how to play 4/4 (that's what all the pop songs I had practiced with were set to). Needless to say, practice went horribly. We ended up cutting the songs that were in 3/4 for the actual service. And after service, they cut me from the worship band. Thankfully my church still let me play for them on Sunday mornings (except for songs that had a 3/4 time signature).

I had natural rhythm and could perform a double kick on my single bass drum pedal — something nearly impossible for younger drummers to accomplish. I could even twirl my drumsticks in between beats. I was a drummer. But, I was also a drummer learning how to drum. Seeing myself as a drummer gave me the confidence to learn how to be a better drummer.

Being able to see ourselves (our mindsets) the same way God sees us gives us the confidence to do what He calls us to do (our behaviors). I'm reminded of the story in the book of Judges when the Holy Spirit speaks to a man named Gideon (Judges 6:11-17). Gideon is hiding some wheat from an approaching army when he hears the Holy Spirit tell him that he will be the one to deliver Israel from the enemy. Gideon questioned this command: "How can I do this thing?"

I love God's response. "Go in this might of yours and save Israel."

The Holy Spirit was asking Gideon to see himself as more than he thought he was, and to do more than he thought he could do.

Our response to the truth of our identity and what God asks of us is often similar to Gideon's. We look at our circumstances and our misdeeds and think we can't possibly be who God says we are and do what He asks us to do. The reality is, we are children of our Heavenly Father and we can do what He says we can do. Our responsibility is to trust God for that identity and allow the Holy Spirit to direct our activity.

God designed us to be in relationship with Him. Unfortunately, we break relationship with the Heavenly Father through distrust, mistrust, and misdeeds, and we need to be reconciled to Him. This takes place through receiving His forgiveness and our repentance. It is through this reconciliation that our mindsets and behaviors begin the process of being redeemed — seeing ourselves and agreeing with how God sees us.

Throughout the Scriptures, the writers use different terms or ideas to communicate this reconciliation and redemptive process. Some examples include: "born again,"[1] "adoption,"[2] "sanctification,"[3] "renewed,"[4] an "heir,"[5] "transformed,"[6] "new creation,"[7] "new self,"[8] "salvation,"[9] "regeneration,"[10] "made alive,"[11] etc. Regardless of the words used, the big idea remains the same; we are reconciled with the Heavenly Father but are in process of being renewed through the Holy Spirit — essentially, we are redeemed and we are being redeemed.

As we walk in step with the Holy Spirit, we trust Him above our emotions, abilities, authority, desires, and experiences. It is through this trust that we develop healthy mindsets and behaviors called "fruit." This fruit is not produced by us "trying harder" or "doing better." It is the natural by-product of resting in the Holy Spirit.[12] Over time, these lifestyles will replace our old, unnatural, self-focused, self-protecting, and self-reliant habits.

The Heavenly Father desires us to live how He designed us to live. Therefore, He will prune from our thoughts and lives anything that chokes out our ability to hear and respond to His Spirit.[13] **Pruning** is *the process of removing dead, fruitless, or unnecessary attitudes, thoughts, habits, or beliefs from our life.* While God may not be organizing every frustrating person or painful circumstance in our life, He will use them to prune us. This is how He renews our mind and empowers us to grow healthy fruit.[14]

---

[1] John 3:3, 7; 1 Peter 1:3, 23
[2] Romans 8:15, 23; 9:4; Galatians 4:5; Ephesians 1:5
[3] Acts 20:32; 26:18; Romans 6:19, 22; 15:16; 1 Corinthians 1:2, 30; 6:11; 1 Thessalonians 4:3; 5:23; 2 Thessalonians 2:13; Hebrews 2:11; 10:10, 14, 29; 13:12; 1 Peter 1:2
[4] Romans 12:2; 2 Corinthians 4:16; Ephesians 4:23; Colossians 3:10; Titus 3:5
[5] Romans 8:17; Galatians 3:29; 4:7; Ephesians 3:6; Titus 3:7; James 2:5; 1 Peter 3:7
[6] Romans 12:2; 2 Corinthians 3:18
[7] 2 Corinthians 5:17; Galatians 6:15
[8] Ephesians 4:24; Colossians 3:10
[9] Ephesians 1:13; 1 Thessalonians 5:9; 2 Timothy 2:10; 3:15; Titus 2:11; Hebrews 2:10; 5:9; 1 Peter 1:9-10; 2:2; Revelation 12:10
[10] Titus 3:5
[11] 1 Corinthians 15:22; Ephesians 2:5; Colossians 2:13
[12] See Galatians 5:16-17
[13] See John 15:1-11
[14] See Romans 12:1-3; 2 Corinthians 4:7-18; Ephesians 4:20-24; Colossians 3:1-10; Titus 3:5

The following[15] are some of the mindsets and behaviors (i.e., "fruit") Paul writes about in his letter to the church in Galatia (Galatians 5:22-26). We can expect to see this fruit when we listen to the Holy Spirit's voice and live empowered by Him.

Fruit of: "Love" (or Preferring Others)

Love is *the denial of ourselves — our rights, desires, beliefs, and expectations — for the benefit of others.* Love prefers others without coercion, compulsion, expectation, manipulation, or requirement. It does not delight in the punishment or negative consequences of those who may deserve them. Rather it hopes for the best outcome.

Fruit of: "Joy" (or Being Delightful)

Joy is *a contentment not based upon circumstances.* This is a hope-filled response to negative, unfair, or unmerited painful circumstances. It acknowledges our limited perspective while trusting God's good character and desire for us.

Fruit of: "Peace" (or Remaining Calm)

Peace is *the capacity to stay calm and composed.* It is a soothing composure amidst relationships or circumstances that are tumultuous, consuming, or offensive. Not emotionally driven or dramatic, peace desires to resolve conflict in a mutually beneficial and harmonious manner.

Fruit of: "Patience" (or Enduring Suffering)

Patience is *an outlook that endures uncertainty with hope.* Patience focuses on and rejoices in the outcome of difficult circumstances rather than the source and details of those circumstances. It is not necessarily the ability to wait, but rather how we act while we wait.

---

[15] The words used come from the ESV translation of the Bible. The descriptions come from the Greek word meanings, synonyms, and use of the word in other Biblical contexts.

Fruit of: "Kindness" (or Experiencing Compassion)

Kindness is *empathy combined with generosity toward other's plight.* This is the ability to understand and share the feelings of someone amidst their deserved or undeserved misfortune or suffering. Additionally, when able, it moves to alleviate any pain or discomfort of the one suffering.

Fruit of: "Goodness" (or Being Beneficial)

Goodness is *provisional help and support toward other's needs.* It strives to meet the needs of others in a meaningful and lasting manner, going beyond simply identifying the specific genuine need.

Fruit of: "Faithfulness" (or Being Trustworthy)

Faithfulness is *characteristically consistent and reliable behavior.* It is the harmony of one's reputation (outward words and actions) and integrity (inward thoughts and motives) in their schedule, finances, relationships, work, morality, judgement, etc.

Fruit of: "Gentleness" (or Not Being Forceful)

Gentleness is *restfully encouraging and strengthening behavior.* It is the capacity to think, communicate, and act with understanding and concern for the well-being of others in a life-giving manner.

Fruit of: "Self-Control" (or Unwavering)

Self-Control is *resistant to coercion, expectation, compulsion, manipulation, or temptation.* It confidently trusts and rests in God's character, plan, and design despite consequences or outcomes.

Paul concludes his discussion of the Holy Spirit's fruit with the understanding that it wasn't an exhaustive list. He ends his list by saying "such things" are the fruit of habitually seeking the Holy Spirit and responding to His guidance. Literally he is saying that these types of mindsets and behaviors, *and those like them*, are how He designed us to live.

When we walk in step with the Holy Spirit, we will live how God originally intended for us to live. These "such things" can be any godly characteristic; that is, anything that is true, honorable, just, pure, lovely, commendable, excellent, praise-worthy, etc.[16] Essentially, it is any attitude, thought, belief, or behavior that is in line with God's character, design, and leading.

Our ability to be healthy and whole — living with peace and rest — is not dependent upon our relationships. However, this peace and rest can dramatically improve our relationships as we release control of what we think should happen. This release will invite healthy fruit to be produced in our life. It is from this healthy fruit that we influence those around us. As we begin to see ourselves for who God created us to be, we will be able to see others the same way and respond to their pain, hurt, and offense with the same love, hope, encouragement, and grace God has given us.

You are designed for relationship — to feel loved, cared for, and safe. But you are also learning how to be in relationship — to grow and mature with God and others. My desire for you is that you would see and experience God's love and care for you — knowing deeply that He truly desires good for you. My hope for you is that you would carry that love, care, and desire for good into every relationship you have.

---

[16] See 1 Corinthians 13:1-13; Philippians 4:8; 1 Timothy 4:7-8; 6:11

the
FREEDOM
booklet

Cultivate

"If you grow a healthy tree, you'll pick healthy fruit. If you grow a diseased tree, you'll pick worm-eaten fruit. The fruit tells you about the tree... A good person produces good deeds and words season after season. An evil person is a blight on the orchard."

— MATTHEW 12:33-35, THE MESSAGE

YOUR LIFE IS LIKE A TREE. YOU CAN PRODUCE HEALTHY FRUIT THAT BENEFITS PEOPLE OR UNHEALTHY FRUIT THAT HURTS PEOPLE.

We are created in the image of God. This identity is intrinsic. Unfortunately, our perception of this identity has been distorted and devalued. Because of this false perception, our heart and mind have been poisoned with negative attitudes, thoughts, beliefs, and feelings. This poison affects our view of God and others. As a result, we cope by fighting or guarding against being hurt. However, these behaviors become habits that poison others while perpetuating our own pain. Only Jesus can redeem our deep-rooted negative perception of our identity — empowering us to enjoy life and live connected with others.

Our lives are like a tree. The fruit of our lives — our behaviors and actions — are fed by the root system of our attitudes, thoughts, beliefs, and feelings. These originate early in our developmental years through our experiences and relationships. If these experiences and relationships are healthy, we develop healthy attitudes, thoughts, beliefs, and feelings that produce healthy coping behaviors and habits. However, if our experience or relationships do not foster healthy attitudes, thoughts, beliefs, or feelings, we develop destructive coping behaviors and habits. Unfortunately, we have all been involved in some form of unhealthy experience or relationship in our early growing up years.

———————— // ————————

This portion of the book comes from *The Freedom Booklet*, a resource that can help you identify and uproot those unhealthy attitudes, thoughts, beliefs, and feelings. It will encourage you to acknowledge the negative effects, repent of your reactions, and release the offender to the Lord. At the end, you will have the opportunity to replace the negative attitudes, thoughts, beliefs, and feelings with God's truth about who you are and about your situation. This truth will empower you to live free in your future no matter what.

As you make your way through this process, I recommend you watch the tutorial videos for each section. These videos can be found at our website:

www.CultivateRelationships.com/Resources

You will find the tutorial videos for this chapter under *The Freedom Booklet* resource.

One final note, I recommend using a notebook or journal to write out your responses to the questions in each section. Writing out your responses will help you clarify your thoughts and bring finality to the process. Also, some of the questions may refer to a response you previously gave. Therefore, writing these answers out will help you reference these responses and bring a thoroughness to the process.

My desire for you as you work through this chapter is that you would be honest with yourself and open for what God may have for you. While some sections in this chapter may be easier than others, I ask that you push through to the end.

STEP 1: EXPERIENCES & RELATIONSHIPS

Examine me, O Lord, and try me; Test my mind and my heart.
~ Psalm 26:2, NASB

Then [Jesus] said to the disciples, "It is impossible
that no offenses should come…"
~ Luke 17:1

Identify areas of offense, hurt, or loss in your life. If this is your first time going through this resource, use the people and offenses you wrote down in the activation step at the end of chapter two. Otherwise, we recommend identifying experiences that happened early in your growing up years.[1] In either case, try to be as specific as possible in the person(s) or situation involved.

The following are some examples of offenses or hurts that you may have experienced in your life:

- *A person's words or actions that made you feel insulted, humiliated, devalued, or rejected.*
- *People or situations where you have been or felt violated or abused.*
- *A separation or divorce in either your own life or in the life of a couple close to you.*
- *Conflicts in your life involving parents, family, friends, coworker, church leaders, mentors, teachers, coaches, or others.*
- *Significant moments where you did not feel loved or safe.*

---

[1] **Forgiving Yourself:** If you feel the need to forgive yourself, you can still benefit from this chapter. Work through this chapter paying special attention to *Step 6: Repenting & Confessing.* Trusting that Jesus has paid this price for your sin — acknowledging and receiving His forgiveness — will empower you to live free of guilt and shame.

Forgiving God or **Processing a Loss:** Processing a loss, unless resulting from one's own choices, is an issue of trusting God and releasing the effects of that loss to Him. If you feel a perceived debt in which God owes you something, you can still benefit from this chapter. Work through this booklet but pay special attention to *Step 9: Receiving & Replacing.* Trusting the Heavenly Father's perfect love, goodness, and character will help you embrace His plan and purpose for your life.

(1.1) Take a few moments to write down as many offenses or hurts that you have experienced in your life.

The following are some examples of significant losses that you may have experienced in your life:

- *Loss of a career or job*
- *Loss of health*
- *Loss of a relationship due to conflict, separation, divorce, or death*
- *Loss of a dream for your life or your future involving relationships, marriage, children, or career, etc.*

(1.2) Write down some significant losses that you experienced in your life.

Choose ONE of the previous offenses, hurts, or losses that you've written down to work through at this time. Again, if this is your first time going through this resource, we recommend using the people and offenses you wrote down in the activation step at the end of chapter two. Otherwise, we recommend choosing one of the earliest experiences or relationships that you identified — especially those relating to your early growing up years in general and your biological parents in particular. These early painful experiences are often where negative attitudes, thoughts, beliefs, and feelings began.

(1.3) Write down the offense, hurt, or loss you are choosing to work through.

(1.4) Write down the offending person that is primarily responsible for this offense, hurt, or loss.

STEP 2: ATTITUDES, THOUGHTS, BELIEFS, & FEELINGS

Search me, O God, and know my heart;
test me and know my anxious thoughts.
~ Psalm 139:23-24, NLT

Early painful experiences and relationships build the foundation of our attitudes, thoughts, beliefs, and feelings. Your willingness to identify these negative attitudes, thoughts, beliefs, and feelings is an important step in becoming free from destructive coping behaviors and habits.

(2.1) Take some time to write down what your thoughts have been regarding the situation.

(2.2) Write down what your thoughts have been toward the person (or people) involved.

Use the following list of words to help clarify, guide, direct, and articulate your thoughts and feelings regarding the specific experience. Identify the top three or four feelings that most apply to you in this specific circumstance.

Unloved	Inadequate	Controlled	Anxious	Unwanted
Unworthy	Not Good Enough	Vulnerable	Resentful	Rejected
Worthless	Frustrated	Unaccepted	Betrayed	Helpless
Insignificant	Out of Control	Unheard	Used	Unsafe
Alone	Not Measuring Up	Invalidated	Victimized	Insecure
Devalued	Unknown	Abandoned	Condemned	Disconnected
Defective	Discouraged	Hopeless	Dirty	Distrust
Shameful	Trapped	Fearful	Powerless	Disrespected
Inferior	Unprotected	Judged	Failure	**Bitter/Anger** [2]

Answer the following questions using the three or four attitudes, thoughts, beliefs, and feelings you've identified above that best fit the way you have felt about the situation or person.

(2.3) Write out how this specific experience has affected you. Be sure to answer separately for each on you identified.
(For example, you may write down: *"I feel ___ because…"*)

---

[2] Bitterness and anger are internal and external behavioral reactions. While we may genuinely "feel" bitter or angry, these are reactions to something or someone triggering a negative emotion is us. If you identified bitterness or anger as your feeling, be sure to include details of these as specific responses in *Step 3: Coping Behaviors & Habits*.

(2.4) Write out how this experience particularly affected your life in a negative way.

(2.5) Write out the emotional, physical, or mental consequences of this experience that you are living with.

(2.6) Write out how this experience has or might negatively affect your future.

(2.7) Write out how this experience has or might negatively affect those you love.

STEP 3: COPING BEHAVIORS & HABITS

Good people bring good things out of the good they store in their hearts.
But evil people bring evil things out of the evil they stored in their hearts.
People speak the things that are in their hearts.
~ Luke 6:45, NLT

We develop destructive coping behaviors and habits when we have believed a lie about ourselves, others, and God; we negatively react to the people that have caused us pain. This begins a lifestyle of fighting or guarding against being hurt again.

(3.1) Write down the things you've said to or about the person or circumstance.

(3.2) Write down things you've done or failed to do to the person or because of them or the circumstance.

(3.3) Write down the thoughts you've had toward the person or about the circumstance.

(3.4) Write down the beliefs you started to have as a result of this offense, specifically toward:

    a. **The Offender**

    b. **The Situation**

(3.5) Write down the beliefs you started to have as a result of this offense, specifically toward:

    a. **Yourself**

    b. **God**

    c. **Similar Situations**

    d. **Similar People** (as the offender)

STEP 4: NEEDS & DESIRES

People, trust God all the time.
Tell him all your problems, because God is our protection.
~ Psalm 62:8, NCV

I cry out to the LORD; I pray to the LORD for mercy.
I pour out my problems to him; I tell him my troubles.
~ Psalm 142:1-2, NCV

We are born with needs and desires. These include being loved, cared for, and safe. In the following responses you will identify and express your unmet needs or desires along with your current ones.

(4.1) Write down how you feel about this person and the situation.

(4.2) Write down what you are disappointed or upset about or what you wish would have happened (or not happened).

(4.3) As you begin to move forward, write down your current needs and desires (what you would like to happen).

STEP 5: GIVE THANKS

I will give thanks to the LORD with my whole heart;
I will recount all your wonderful deeds.
~ Psalm 9:1, ESV

I will offer to you the sacrifice of thanksgiving,
and will call upon the name of the LORD.
~ Psalm 116:17, NKJV

Always give thanks to God the Father for everything,
in the name of the Lord Jesus Christ.
~ Ephesians 5:20, NCV

Giving thanks to God aligns our perspective with His. It helps us begin to trust Him amidst painful experiences — releasing control of what we think should happen. However, this can be very difficult and often feels like a sacrifice. Ask God to help you find something to be thankful for regarding the experience and tell Him in writing. Finally, tell Him that you are willing to accept however He wants to use this circumstance in your life.

(5.1) Write down your prayer of thanksgiving to God.

THE SERVANT WHO NEVER FORGAVE.

Then Peter came to [Jesus] and asked, "Lord, how often should I forgive someone who sins against me? Seven times?"

"No, not seven times," Jesus replied, "but seventy times seven!

"Therefore, the Kingdom of Heaven can be compared to a king who decided to bring his accounts up to date with servants who had borrowed money from him. In the process, one of his debtors was brought in who owed him millions of dollars. He couldn't pay, so his master ordered that he be sold—along with his wife, his children, and everything he owned—to pay the debt.

"But the man fell down before his master and begged him, 'Please, be patient with me, and I will pay it all.' **Then his master was filled with pity for him, and he released him and forgave his debt.**

"But when the man left the king, he went to a fellow servant who owed him a few thousand dollars. **He grabbed him by the throat and demanded instant payment.**

"His fellow servant fell down before him and begged for a little more time. 'Be patient with me, and I will pay it,' he pleaded. But his creditor wouldn't wait. He had the man arrested and put in prison until the debt could be paid in full.

"When some of the other servants saw this, they were very upset. They went to the king and told him everything that had happened. Then the king called in the man he had forgiven and said, 'You evil servant! **I forgave you that tremendous debt because you pleaded with me. Shouldn't you have mercy on your fellow servant, just as I had mercy on you?'** Then the angry king sent the man to prison to be tortured until he had paid his entire debt.

"That's what my heavenly Father will do to you if you refuse to forgive your brothers and sisters from your heart."

— MATTHEW 18:21-35 | NLT *Emphasis Added*

STEP 6: REPENTING & CONFESSING

*Pain handled in God's way produces a turning from sin to God which
leads to salvation, and there is nothing to regret in that! But pain handled in
the world's way produces only death. For just look at what handling the pain
God's way produced in you! What earnest diligence, what eagerness to clear
yourselves, what indignation, what fear, what longing, what zeal,
what readiness to put things right! In everything you have
proved yourselves blameless in the matter.*
~ 2 Corinthians 7:10-11, CJB

*But if we confess our sins, he will forgive our sins, because we can trust God to
do what is right. He will cleanse us from all the wrongs we have done.*
~ 1 John 1:9, NCV

*Make this your common practice: Confess your sins to each other and pray for
each other so that you can live together whole and healed.*
~ James 5:16, THE MESSAGE

Repentance is turning away from our own desires and lifestyles
toward God, to live how He designed us to live. It is full
acknowledgement, trust, and submission to the Heavenly Father
and His design and plan for our life. Finish the following
statements of confession and repentance in your journal or
notebook.

**(6.1) Write down your confession and statement of
repentance for your unwillingness to forgive the
offending person.**

(6.2) Write down your apology for what you've said and done toward the person that were wrong, hurtful, or negative. (Refer to Step 3, questions 1-2.)

(6.3) Write down your apology for the wrong, hurtful, or negative thoughts and attitudes you've believed or decisions you've made. (Refer to Step 3, questions 3-4.)

(6.4) Write down your apology for the wrong, hurtful, or negative thoughts and attitudes you've believed or decisions you made. (Refer to Step 3, question 5.)

(6.5) Write down the summation of your apology. Confess and repent to the Holy Spirit for all the thoughts and behaviors you've been living out of. Finally, end your apology thanking God for His goodness, faithfulness, and His forgiveness.

STEP 7: FORGIVING OFFENSES

Yes, if you forgive others their sins, your Father in heaven
will also forgive you for your sins. But if you don't forgive others,
your Father in heaven will not forgive your sins.
~ Matthew 6:14-15, NCV

Make a clean break with all cutting, backbiting, profane talk.
Be gentle with one another, sensitive. Forgive one another as
quickly and thoroughly as God in Christ forgave you.
~ Ephesians 4:31-32, NCV

Answer the following statements by writing out your decision to forgive the person who has sinned against you. Forgive the specific hurts or offenses, releasing your control to God. Choose to forgive the person who has hurt or offended you. Include the specific consequences of how they have negatively affected you in the past. Also, include how they are currently affecting you, and may affect you in the future. One last note, if you feel like you still need to forgive yourself, revisit Step 6, answering the questions (especially 2-5). Then skip to Step 8 and entrust your sin along with any negative consequences on others or yourself to God — trusting Jesus has paid the price for your sin and embrace His forgiveness.

If you are processing a loss, remember that God's perfect love and infinite goodness exclude Him from being forgiven. Processing a loss is often an issue of trusting God's love and goodness amidst disappointment or tragedy. If you feel as though God still "owes" you something, look back at Step 6 and answer questions 4 and 5. Then, skip to Step 8 and entrust yourself and your circumstances to His love and goodness.

In your notebook or journal, write out and complete the following statements with your own words.

(7.1) I choose to forgive _____ for the following offense...

(7.2) I am choosing to forgive _____ for the following ways this offense has affected me in the past. (Refer to Step 2, question 3.)

(7.3) I am choosing to forgive _____ for the following ways this offense has affected me in my current circumstances and relationships. (Refer to Step 2, question 4.)

(7.4) I am choosing to forgive _____ for the following foreseen and unforeseen ways this offense may affect me in my future. (Refer to Step 2, question 5.)

(7.5) I am choosing to forgive _____ for the following foreseen and unforeseen ways this offense has affected those I love. (Refer to Step 2, question 6.)

STEP 8: RELEASING & BLESSING

"I'm telling you to love your enemies. Let them bring out the best in you,
not the worst. When someone gives you a hard time, respond with the
energies of prayer, for then you are working out of your true selves,
your God-created selves. This is what God does."
~ Matthew 5:44-45, THE MESSAGE

Don't hit back; discover beauty in everyone. If you've got it in you,
get along with everybody. Don't insist on getting even; that's not for you to do.
"I'll do the judging," says God. "I'll take care of it." Our scripture tells us
that if you see your enemy hungry, go buy that person lunch, or if he's thirsty,
get him a drink. Your generosity will surprise him with goodness.
Don't let evil get the best of you; get the best of evil by doing good.
~ Romans 12:17-21, THE MESSAGE

This is one of the most powerful steps in forgiveness — letting go of your control and desired outcomes. God is faithful. He is bigger and better at dealing with our offenses and disappointments. Give control back to Him so that He can do something good with it — so that His grace can relieve your pain and anxiety.

If you're going through this resource for a sin you've committed, then you can be confident that you are forgiven through Jesus' death on the cross. You simply receive and live confidently knowing you are loved and the pain and disappointment you've caused others can be remedied. Entrust your thoughts, behaviors, and current circumstances to God's grace and mercy — allow Him to free you of shame, guilt, and condemnation.

If you're working through this resource grieving the loss of someone or something, know that God can work horribly traumatic circumstances out for your good. Because of our limited perspective, we do not get to define what that good may mean. He may not have caused the circumstance, but He will fix the circumstance to bring peace and hope back into your mind and life. We release control and what we think should have happened to God's perfect love, grace, mercy, and goodness.

In your notebook or journal, write out and complete the following statements with your own words. If you're repenting, entrust yourself and the consequences to God. Ask Him to specifically bless the negative circumstances you've caused and/or the people you've hurt. If you're grieving, entrust the circumstance to God. Ask Him to redeem and remedy the pain, loss, and anxiety you're feeling.

(8.1) I choose to release _____ to You good Father, in the following specific ways.

(8.2) I am choosing to pray over _____ the following specific blessings — asking that You would make the following good things happen in their life...

STEP 9: RECEIVING & REPLACING

*Then Jesus said to those Jews who believed Him, "If you abide in My word,
you are My disciples indeed. And you shall know the truth,
and the truth shall make you free."*
~ John 8:31-32, NKJV

Despite what you have done or what has been done to you, God desires to redeem your true identity — removing your distorted and devalued perception of yourself. Prayerfully go through the next step, asking the Holy Spirit to speak truth to you about who you are and who He is. Pray through the following prayers. Then, in your journal or notebook write down what He speaks to you or shows you. While it may take a few moments to clearly hear His voice, it will often be the first thing that comes to your mind after you pray. Trust that this is His voice.

"Heavenly Father, thank You for desiring good for me. I trust that You will speak to me and that Your voice will be clear."

(9.1) *"Holy Spirit, because of this circumstance or relationship, what LIE have I believed about myself?"*
(Before continuing, write down what you heard or saw.)

(9.2) *"Holy Spirit, because of this circumstance or relationship, what LIE have I believed about You?"*
(Before continuing, write down what you heard or saw.)

(9.3) *"Holy Spirit, what TRUTH do you want me to believe about myself?"* (Before continuing, write down what you heard or saw.)

(9.4) *"Holy Spirit, what TRUTH do you want me to believe about You?"* (Before continuing, write down what you heard or saw.)

(9.5) *"Jesus, I choose to give you the LIE that I am..."* (Picture yourself handing Jesus the lie from 9.1.)

(9.6) *"Jesus, I choose to replace the LIE with the TRUTH that I am..."* (Picture Jesus handing you the truth from 9.3.)

(9.7) *"Jesus, I choose to give you the LIE that the Heavenly Father is..."* (Picture yourself handing Jesus the lie from 9.2.)

(9.8) *"Jesus, I choose to replace the LIE with the TRUTH that the Heavenly Father is..."* (Picture Jesus handing you the truth from 9.4.)

FINAL ENCOURAGEMENT

Share with a close friend or family member what you've worked through — talking through what you wrote down in your journal or notebook (e.g., your responses, thoughts, feelings, and prayers). Being vulnerable with this *Encouragement Partner* will enhance the freedom and experience of this resource. This will encourage you to keep moving forward in forgiveness and pursuing wholeness.

Then, celebrate with that person. Celebrate the win this process has brought to your life. Get ice cream, go out for dinner, whatever it is. Celebrate!

When you've thoroughly celebrated, go through this process again, dealing with another person or offense. Continue revisiting this resource every time you feel anxious, frustrated, discouraged, or hurt by someone. Continue to write down your responses to these steps in a journal or notebook. Each journal or notebook will become a trophy of freedom — a symbol of what God is doing in your life and relationships.

Discuss each one with an *Encouragement Partner.*

Then, celebrate each one.

Made in the USA
Monee, IL
12 November 2020